The Shaman's Lover Trilogy

Book I

the spell

praise for

The Shaman's Lover Trilogy

Book I

the Spell

"If you've ever been curious about Ayahuasca and the Shamanic journey, look no further. In this no-frills autobiographical account, *The Spell*, Book One of *The Shaman's Lover's Trilogy*, catapults us down the rabbit hole of spiritual "sex, drugs and rock 'n roll" into the heart of one woman's search for authenticity, self-empowerment and self-love. In her relentless intention to leave nothing unexplored, Georgina Kemm has created a compelling and naked reveal of both her inner workings and her fearless dive into this veiled jungle world. By the end, the veil has been lifted. And what remains is a fascination with our own longing for self-discovery."

-ASHARA LYNN GORBET

"*The Spell* is a deeply honest true story. Georgina invites us all in to a no-holds barred, genuine journey with her through the mystery of Amazonian shamanism, the Mother Jungle and the depths of our desires and motivations. A true invitation to dive deep in to the many shades of seduction, sorcery, friendship, power and the depths of one woman's heart."

-SYLVIE JOY MEIER, Shaman-ayahuasquera, Carrier of the Sacred Medicine, Kambo and owner of *https://www.loscielosperu.com/*

"*The Spell* is Book I of *The Shaman's Lover Trilogy*, a story of one woman's search for the secrets of her own essence by way of Africa, Santa Fe, New Mexico and the Amazon jungle of Peru. Author Georgina Kemm's honest and powerful voice pulls us moment by moment into a remarkable tale of betrayal, unfolding self-knowledge, and mystical power.

The Spell will have you turning the pages as the main character is drawn across continents and into the depths of herself through mystic visions and the irresistible spell of magic love."

-ERNESTINE B COLUMBO, author of #1 Amazon Bestseller, *Returning Souls*

"Oh my God! Wow, *The Spell* is amazing! I love it! Thank you for letting me read your story. I'm not a reader and was captured and compelled to take in the whole thing. Georgina Kemm writes a beautiful, bold expression of being human through her transparency. She shares her pain, suffering, longing and the courage to embrace self-honesty and healing. Ultimately, she opens us up to the freedom to our greater authenticity. A profound gift of heart-opening and self-love to all who read it."

-RIELLE PELLETIER, Relationship and Intimacy Coach-
https://iliveempowered.com/

"*The Spell* is for the truth seeker. Georgina Kemm has coupled her raw and fast moving writing style with vivid details of the senses—keeping you in pace with every word of this page-turner memoir. Mysteries of your own life peel away and reveal hidden meaning as you witness this fascinating wise woman's expedition of the complex yet common journey of the feminine essence. This feminine essence is coming up for air in all of us. Her tale takes you on a trek through arid high deserts to lush sugary beaches to dense jungles laden with life. As you read, you may question what is real or what are just dreams and visions, and be confronted with the thrilling or even horrifying possibility that it is ALL real. I want more of these books!"

-SALLY REEVES CONWAY, Director of Coaching,
The Art of Feminine Presence™

The Shaman's Lover Trilogy

Book I

the spell

by
Georgina Lucy Kemm

Copyright © 2018 by Georgina Lucy Kemm

All rights reserved.

No part of this book may be reproduced in any form or by any electronic or mechanical means including storage and retrieval systems, without permission in writing from the author. The only exception is by a reviewer, who may quote short excerpts in a review. Scanning, uploading and electronic distribution of this book or the facilitation of such without permission from the author is prohibited. Please purchase only authorized electronic editions, and do not participate in or encourage electronic piracy of copyrighted material. Your support of the author's rights is appreciated.

Cover concept & design by: Georgina Kemm, germancreative @ Fiverr.com

Front Cover Images: Keller Welten and Mohamed Hassan from Pixaby.com

Back Cover Images: Mohamed Hassan @ Pixaby.com & depositphoto.com

Back Page Author Photograph: Oscar Lozoya

This is a Non-fiction Memoir.
I have recreated events, locales and conversations based on my journal writings from the time of these events and my memories of them. In some instances, names of individuals have been changed in order to maintain their anonymity and protect their privacy.

Written by Georgina Lucy Kemm
www.theShamansLover.com
Printed in the United States of America -
First Printing:
Published by: Sojourn Publishing, LLC
Published for: Sacred Medicine Society, LLC

Paperback ISBN: 978-1-62747-266-1
Ebook ISBN: 978-1-62747-268-5

To Mama Aya,
for bringing me back to Life.

gratitude

To my loving husband Damian for his infinite support as he waited patiently for me to bring this book into manifestation. My plant medicine teachers and the beautiful Amazon jungle for providing the space in which I could heal. Denise Cassino for believing in me, holding my hand, and giving me endless amounts of encouragement to keep going. Tom Bird for telling me "it's time" and providing the map to travel the road for the completion and publication of this book. John Hodgkinson, the project coordinator for linearizing my very right-brain. Ernie Columbo, a fellow author; for her generosity and kindness. Sylvie Joy Meier, my shaman friend and her intimate knowledge of *plantas amorosas* and understanding the hidden magic between the words I wrote. Gennaro Ambrosino for permission to use his photos. To the lovely women who have read my story and wrote beautiful responses. And, with the deepest gratitude, to all the characters in this book who were once part of my life. Without you, I wouldn't be who I am today.

preface

"...It doesn't interest me how old you are. I want to know if you will risk looking like a fool for love, for your dreams, for the adventure of being alive..."
Oriah Mountain Dreamer, from The Invitation

The Shaman's Lover Trilogy has been hiding in my laptop since I wrote the initial draft in 2010. I imagine other authors must go through similar experiences of fear and self-doubt as to whether the story is worth telling at all. Especially, something as vulnerable as a memoir – I was dragged back through time and space to relive the experiences over and over until I reached a place of neutrality and peace.

This story includes some very visceral, visionary experiences with the powerful plant medicine, ayahuasca, interspersed with my life and relationships as I experienced them at the time. As you are reading, you may feel as if you have been transported to another world, perhaps sparking a deeper, multi-dimensional curiosity about yourself. I always say to people when someone asks me about ayahuasca, "It's for either the brave or crazy, or perhaps you have to be both." However, through this book you will receive the medicine you are meant to receive in a much gentler, kinder way than I did.

To preserve and transfer the authentic flavor of my experience, I have chosen to maintain a number of words in the local languages as I have learned them. Additionally, I haven't changed the names of the plants or animals into their scientific names.

The Spell is for you if you have ever given your power away, in the small seemingly inconsequential ways of saying "yes" when you meant "no" or in big ways, like I did. This book is for you if you have felt the hollowness of low self-worth, yearning to fill up your empty vessel with love, freedom, your truth, and claim your power. This book is for you if you have felt stuck, dissatisfied, or desperate. And, this book is for all of you who just know in the marrow of your bones, you could be more, so much more, if only you could tell your story in all your humanness and be heard. *The Spell* will inspire you to live unapologetically in your feminine essence and beauty and to love fearlessly, especially yourself.

Love,
Georgina Lucy Kemm

chapter one

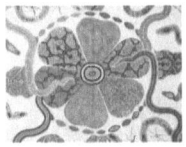

The water, almost cool now, reminds me how long I've been here.

I reach for the tap, letting the hot flowing water burn my toes.

The CD player rests on the top of the toilet tank. The magic songs of the Amazon reach through the speakers and wrap around me like vines, bringing up an intense longing that makes everything else impossible to bear.

As the candle starts to flicker, I slide my right forearm across the bathtub's cool porcelain lip, fumbling for the smooth resin handle.

I grab hold of it, hanging on tightly to the part of me I'm afraid to lose.

I sink beneath the hot water like an anaconda sliding from the muddy bank into a river.

Minutes later, I burst through the surface. Gasping, I gulp down the cool spring air, putting out the fire in my lungs.

My breathing returns to its shallow rhythm and I pick up the sharp metal tip and jab it into my index finger. A crimson drop drifts like paint, staining the water's surface. I watch it swirl and spiral as it loses itself on the bottom of the tub. I stick my finger tip in my mouth, tasting the metallic life force.

The handle, now warm, seems less foreign and almost a part of me. I lift the knife and let it land heavily across my wrist, intersecting the roads of tendons and veins. Stale breath rushes from my lips and the candle sitting in the corner sputters and nearly dies.

March 2008, less than a month earlier.

I wasn't even aware of what was going on in the USA, never mind the world. I was totally absorbed in my own little galaxy. It began to tumble and tumble some more, until one day, I found myself buried in a pile of rubble, and it certainly wasn't star dust.

The housing bubble whispered collapse.

The real estate broker did his best to convince me to lower the selling price of our house. I was stubborn, and I agreed to if it didn't sell within the month. By this point, I was fed up with people telling me what to do. And, I had faith in our little house. That it would find the right people to live in it. Just as it had found us four and a half years ago.

I guess we were pretty lucky. Within a week, our house sold and we got our asking price. My husband, Doug, was in Bolivia working. So, we faxed agreements back and forth until the deal was complete.

Doug had abandoned the relationship and left the details of tying up the final strings of it to me. He insisted on keeping everything we owned.

"It doesn't work like that," I reminded him in an email. And I agreed not to sell what he had picked out. He selected a few of the nicest and most expensive items. But I kept my word. I made tags using a red Sharpie. I wrote "sold" on the little papers and taped them to our old Mexican furniture. I didn't want to. But I would feel too guilty if I got overly vindictive.

Even though forest fire rage burned through me.

Last week, the Fed-Ex truck crunched up the gravel driveway, and, dropped off a slim white envelope with Doug's name neatly typed on it.

It might be important. It had arrived while he was away. It might be related to his work in Bolivia, I think. I rip back the paper tab. Curious, I reach my hand inside.

I pull out plane tickets.

Two of them.

Destination: Brazil.

Funny. He never mentioned another trip. June-bugs smack against the walls of my belly.

I scan the names. One in his name. The other, in a woman's name I've never heard of.

My mind helicopters and crashes. I try to put the pieces together. My stomach cramps as the rage rumbles. *No wonder he made a mad dash to move out of the house.*

Now, I understand why he is pushing so hard for the divorce to go through. A net of paranoia catches all reason. I rifle through papers on the counter, searching for the credit-card statement. I tear it open it. Scrolling down the list of purchases, I discover an unusual charge. To Yahoo personals, just a month ago. *And he is already taking some woman on a trip, paying for her ticket with our joint credit card!* My brain is about to explode.

I hate him.

I hate myself more for being so stupid.

My eyes cloud red with revenge. I am going to sell everything and keep all the money for myself. I feel justified.

The day of the estate sale can't come fast enough.

chapter two

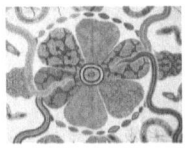

April 2008

I didn't know how much work went into organizing an estate sale.

Thank goodness, my spunky red-headed friend, Jez, helped me lay everything out. Buyers lined up out the front door at seven in the morning even though the sale began at eight. I was already overwhelmed, and we hadn't even begun.

By about nine, it finally hits me as I sell things for a dollar here, five dollars there: little by little, teacup and chair, my old life is disappearing.

The rage turns into sadness I don't understand. I am giving up my life and letting it all go. All the household items are just symbolic of the severing I am doing. My job and financial security, my home, my marriage, and my dogs.

I will have nothing left.

Late that afternoon, Doug's truck sneaks through parked vehicles lining the driveway.

He told me he wouldn't be home until tomorrow. That I wouldn't need to get him from the airport. Another lie. That bitch obviously picked him up.

In his usual style, he tries to commandeer the garage sale. He grabs plates and screwdrivers and knick-knacks right out of potential buyers' hands. He doesn't want to part with anything, and people are walking out.

I stare at him, eyes wide with disbelief.

I am furious but try to keep my cool in front of all the people crowded into the house.

He doesn't know I know about his girlfriend and Brazil.

Jez senses my stress and yells, "Get out of here! You're not being any help. You think you can show up here and run the show? We don't need your help now. The hard work has been done, Doug!"

"But I don't want you selling my stuff," he whines at her. She won't have any of his nonsense and points to the front door.

She looks at me and rolls her eyes. She spins on her heel, jitterbugging her way through the crowd, chatting with buyers.

Like a rash, heat prickles the top of my ears as the taffy-like tension increases in the kitchen. Through clenched teeth, I hoarsely command Doug to go the back bathroom where we can talk in private.

I can't hold it in any longer than it takes me to slam the door.

"I can't believe you bought that bitch tickets and then had them sent here!" I rant, hovering the white business envelope over the toilet bowl. I hold them gingerly between my fingers, letting them drop into the water. I slam the lid down and reach for the flush.

"NO!" he yells, pushing past me and reaching into the toilet to retrieve the soggy tickets. "They weren't supposed to come here."

Whatever! "Why didn't it go to her house or your mom's then? That bitch sent them here on purpose so I would know about her."

His eyes dart left, then quickly cloud over.

"She's not a bitch."

How would he know? He's only known her for a few weeks!

"And where did you find her anyway? The Yahoo Personals?" I smirk in disgust.

His shoulders droop like a shirt falling off the hanger, "So what? It's a good way to meet people." He twists the ring encircling his finger. "And Fred said I should start dating and meet people. So I could get on with my life."

Fred, that's another story.

He is a shaman/metaphysical teacher/hypnotherapist. And my trusted counselor nearly every week for the last six years. He moved in with Doug shortly after he and his partner separated and he needed a place to stay. Apparently, he switched allegiances.

Assholes, both of them.

"Couldn't you have waited at least until we signed the papers? Why didn't you tell her to wait a couple more weeks instead of pulling this shit? You didn't think I would find out?" I fired at him.

"I didn't mean for this to happen. Honestly," he says, looking down at his knotty bunions.

"Get the fuck out. I don't want Jez to be out there by herself the whole time," I shout as I push past him into the darkening hallway.

"Don't sell my stuff!" he yells.

His stupid possessions.

Now, he's got a new one.

"I am selling everything except what you asked for," I shout back over my shoulder.

I ignore him from then on while he is outside doing his best to save face with our friends and neighbors. Eventually he leaves, taking an overflowing armload with him.

What I didn't sell that day, I gave away.

I made enough money to buy myself a plane ticket for wherever I decide to go.

Dusk had darkened the sky by the time Jez gave me a hug good-bye. I wave her off and watch her old white Ford Escape turn the corner and disappear through the junipers.

I walk back through the open door into the barren house. My footsteps bounce through the silence and echo off the bare walls.

There is no sofa left to sit on, only the hard, wooden chairs Doug wants. So, I crumple to the floor like a worn-out pair of jeans. I don't realize how tired I really am, now that I don't have to hold myself together. With no one watching, I coil up like a small voice inside a bottomless cave.

chapter three

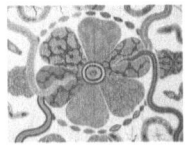

Winter 2007

Doug and I had separated for a while.
But a combination of couple's therapy and a snowstorm brought him back into the house.

Doug came over for dinner one night and within several hours, three feet of snow dumped on the ground, impounding his truck and keeping him at the house for the next three days.

Like a bad habit, we pick up where we left off. I put the marriage back on like an old pair of shoes I had just dug out from the back of the closet.

The only problem is now, they feel tight.

To tell you the truth, I don't know if Doug was always so stingy and telling me what to do, or that I never noticed.

Or perhaps, a few months of space had given me a sense of freedom I could not remember until I had a taste. I jump back into the familiar pattern of my marriage. All the while, harboring dreadful uneasiness in the pit of my stomach, I keep trying to convince myself that this time it will be different.

This time our marriage will work.

A smothering depression slinks upon me. It relaxes its grip when Doug announces that we get to go on a trip to the Seychelles, Mauritius and Zanzibar. The State Department hired him to do conflict resolution workshops there.

How exciting this was!

Georgina Lucy Kemm

    For my ninth birthday, my dad bought me a cardboard world globe. I would spin it incessantly, looking for those tiny dots that were islands. Ever since, I had fantasized about what an exotic life I would lead one day. And how different it would be, compared to life on the farm.

    And, the best thing Doug and I do together is travel. This trip will be like old times, bringing us closer together.

chapter four

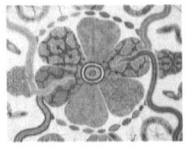

As usual, we fly separately.

Doug flies business class booked by the State Department and paid for with tax dollars.

His last ticket to Africa was over ten thousand dollars. Meanwhile, I travel economy class.

I don't mind the thirty-three hour flight from Albuquerque to the Seychelles Islands near the bottom tip of the African continent. By the time I stop over in Dubai, I am ready to do a little shopping, and I buy three Arabic music CDs. Surprisingly, the several-hour layover goes quickly. Before I know it, I am taking my belt off and going through security and back on the plane to my island destination.

I squish my nose against the faced-sized double pane. I notice the sliver of black sandwiched between the Indian Ocean and the island.

Will the pilot really make the skinny runway? I wonder, as he circles for his second attempt.

With a bounce, the wheels *thud thud thud* as if they were running across a washboard, then finally come to a stop. I walk down the steel steps and across the steamy tarmac that gives off that oily-tar smell. In the toy-sized airport, I wait my turn in line to pass through customs and immigration. An officer with disinterested eyes and a tired-of-tourists smile, writes "14" in the square marked "days" on my visitor visa.

At the conveyor belt, I wait for my backpack to appear.

As I had anticipated, it doesn't show up.

I had double-checked with the agent in New York when I noticed she had only tagged it to Dubai. But, she insisted that my bag would make it all the way. Before I leave the airport, I make a pit-stop at the airline counter and report my lost bag. A perfectly groomed agent in an island sand-yellow uniform assures me my luggage will be transported to my hotel.

Outside, I locate the resort's shuttle bus.

It passes through Victoria, the quaint colonial capitol. Ribboning across the small, hilly island, the bus pulls into the resort's cul-de-sac driveway.

Smiling at paradise, I step out of the van, pausing a moment to inhale the clean, moist air and etch it into my memory. Rafters stretch up, embracing me as I await Doug inside the open-air lobby.

In about half an hour, Doug exits a car, his hair springy with curls due to the humidity. His eyes find me, I smile, and rise to greet him. We hug briefly, and he leads me past a swimming pool to our room on the second floor.

Our compact room feels pleasantly cool. But, I'm hungry from traveling, so we venture to the restaurant down by the pool. We sit under a roof of banana palm fronds and Doug methodically explains his work itinerary to me.

I'm only half listening.

The exquisite turquoise water lures my eyes into it.

I wiggle with impatience, wishing that my swimsuit had made the connection from Dubai. Pria, an orchid flower of a woman with chocolate skin approaches our table. She plants her slender frame on the chair between us.

She and Doug will be working together on the same project. After they finish here, we will then continue onto her island in Mauritius where they will instruct another conflict-resolution workshop.

Doug scoots his chair around to angle himself towards Pria.

A fist of anger punches my stomach.

An outsider in their conversation, I feel invisible.

He is asking her about work and where she went to school. Soon they start gossiping about her boss, and I get lost in the fantasy of swimming in the ocean. Pria calls me back into the conversation, asking me about my work as a massage therapist. We chat a moment before Doug interrupts us with more questions about their schedule.

The lead weight that presses against my heart nails me to the plastic chair.

Finally, Pria announces that she's tired and gets up to leave.

The heaviness of my thoughts follows her out. Anger rushes in to fill the vacuum when Doug comments, "She's really nice, isn't she?"

I brush my feelings aside, suddenly feeling exhausted.

Doug and I walk through the insectile chorus into the humid night and return to our room.

That, at least, overlooks a little piece of heaven.

chapter five

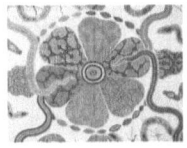

The next day, Doug is at work, leaving me to my own devices.

Luckily my backpack did arrive on yesterday afternoon's final flight from Dubai.

I dig through my neatly rolled clothes and extract my bikini. I put it on, then cover myself with an airy, long-sleeve cotton shirt and a sarong. I weave between white lounging chairs that fringe the pool's edge before I exit the resort's open gate. I quickly feel over-dressed among the mostly naked and bronzed Europeans littered on the powdery white sand.

I swish out my sarong and as soon as it finds a spot to lie on the beach, I drop onto it.

Suddenly, I'm aware of how vanilla I am and decide I could hide better if I sneak into the water.

I march into the shallow water. Lying back, I close my eyes. Like driftwood, I bob upon the waves as time silently dissolves.

My eyes sting.

Time to get out as my skin tightens from the sun-baked salt.

More bravely now, I lie on my belly under the shade of a voluptuous tree.

My ears crunch with sand as I insert the headphones to listen to Pimsleur's Swahili lesson. I gaze out over the turquoise water, observing the distinct line where the turquoise transforms into a deep azure blue. I can see the jade turtleback of another island that belongs to the Seychelles' collection of the one hundred and fifteen tiny dots on the globe.

Dark brown calves and broad feet kick sand onto my sarong.

Annoyed, I stare out onto the water and focus with more effort to Swahili lesson number four on my iPod.

Those chocolatey legs now squat next to me below a happy face and arms hugging his shins. I could see his full lips moving, but I ignore him, pretending I can't hear a word he says.

The plump pout keeps moving.

Deepening the furrows between my eyebrows, I glare at him with even more effort.

He does not leave. After a few minutes of that persistent smile, I feel forced to take out my right ear-bud. I hear him shout, "What are you listening to?"

"*Hujambo!*" Rudely, I say hello in Swahili, looking at him squarely, hoping my arrogance will make him leave.

"*Habari gani*? How are you?" he responds with an impish grin.

A warm, pink flush tingles the top of my ears. Flustered and not so confident, I return his question in English. Curiosity overtakes me, "Where did you learn Swahili?"

"My grandfather came from Kenya, and I learned from him." He smiles warmly at me.

"How did your grandfather get here?" The Seychelles are in the middle of nowhere.

"When he was a young man he came in a boat with three of his friends."

Wanting to know more. "Why did he want to leave Kenya?"

"He was an adventurer. He thought he could make a good life here."

"Wow. That's pretty crazy." Kenya is nearly a thousand miles from here!

I begin to relax under the influence of his friendliness and charm.

Scrutinizing him, I notice his golden-brown eyes set like sun-fire opals inside his beautiful face.

Afraid of having my investigation discovered, I shamefully avert my eyes toward the sand.

Offering me his hand, he says, "My name is Sunley."

I take it and notice the lines of his palm feel like tooled leather against mine. Yes, Sunley is a good name for him. He does look like he has a sunny disposition.

"Would you have dinner with me tonight?" he asks.

What?! How forward of him!

I must admit; I'm flattered by the attention.

"I can't. I'm married!" I say, as if it's his fault.

He shrugs off the rejection like a horse shaking a fly.

Wait! Don't go! I think. Sadly, I watch him rise from a squat and stride away.

He doesn't go far. I spy him several times on the beach. Each time he passes by me, he shouts, "Hello, beautiful Georgina!"

Every time he says, "beautiful," the word acts as an elixir, invigorating and intoxicating me at the same time.

I can't get Sunley out of my head.

It seemed like a long time since someone had called me beautiful.

I like to believe Doug used to think I was beautiful. That was when he thought the world of me.

chapter six

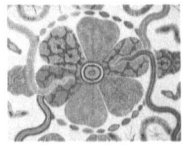

Doug and I met in Quetzaltenango, Guatemala in the early spring of 1996.

I worked at Casa de Español Xelajú, a Spanish-language school as an international coordinator. He taught at one of the local universities.

Doug was a former student at the school and often came by to visit the teachers who had become his friends.

One day, I was in the middle of my five-hour daily Spanish lesson, working on the dreaded subjunctive verbs. I was sitting in one of those straight-backed wooden chairs that didn't give me a choice about good posture when he strutted past me and disappeared down the hallway. He wore a brown and black handwoven embroidered jacket typical of the region. He had a black Columbia messenger bag slung over his shoulder. The flaming mane of his curls bounced unapologetically, drawing me in like a moth.

With a playful smile, he locked my eyes in his gaze. Helpless, I felt my cheeks heat up and turn cherry red.

He never emerged from the back of the school.

Finally, break time arrived. I ventured to the coffee room and saw him looming over the short Guatemalans. Doug leaned into Monica, the woman who was training me, and said something quietly. Suddenly, laughter erupted from the group, and they looked over at me.

"Georgina," Monica called, gesturing me to join the group. "This is Doug," she said. He reached out his slender, freckled hand.

I extended my hand. Nervous and tongue-tied, "Nice to meet you," I responded. I stood there a few seconds feeling rather on the spot and decided I better refill my coffee cup.

"Excuse me." I gave a slight nod and backed out of the circle. I felt his eyes etch into my back as I made my way over to the table displayed with an assortment of breads and the coffee and tea.

At one o'clock, I finished my class and walked back to the house where I was staying for lunch. A couple of the lunch regulars from the school are already digging into their beans, rice and chicken. Doña Olga has just put my plate down when through the doorway I heard, "*Buenas tardes,*" in a vaguely familiar voice.

Doug took the empty seat right next to me. I stared straight into my plate, hoping he didn't notice the crimson creeping across my face. He didn't seem shy at all and jumped right into conversation. I began to relax, laughing a little at the teasing coming from the Guatemalans who obviously sensed the electrical charge between us.

That night, before we were about to finish for the night, Doug appeared and peeked his head into the office.

"Hola," the staff and I chimed.

"Hola," he said as he ducked out into the entrance area.

I felt the tension increase in his presence. I was glad he went to another room so I could have a moment to breathe before I passed by him again. I gathered up my pack and kissed everyone in the office goodbye.

As I made my way toward the door, he moved up next to me. I didn't say anything and let him fill the silence.

"Do you want to go out with me later," which tumbled onto, "If you're not busy tonight, we could go get dinner or something."

"Well, I can't tonight. It's a little late to let Doña Olga know I won't be eating there."

"Yeah, okay." He was kicking a rock with his shoe. "How about tomorrow then? You can let her know in advance."

"Sounds good," I smiled.

He stopped kicking the rock, "How about I meet you here after work?"

"Okay." We parted. "*Hasta mañana*," I called back over my shoulder.

The next night we met. He took me to a tiny restaurant with four square handmade tables. I ordered the vegetable soup and rice. We then split a piece of carrot cake for dessert.

Our conversation meandered as we shared our travel journeys. It didn't take long before it felt as if we were old friends.

It was getting late when Doug asked for the check. The owner sitting at a table in the corner approached us and placed a small white paper face down.

Neither of us reach for it. A few awkward minutes later Doug turned the paper over.

"Do you want to go Dutch?"

Taken aback, "Yeah, I guess so." I wasn't expecting this. I was irritated.

He reached into his front pocket of his jeans and dug out his wallet.

Then like crocodile jaws, he opened it up even further. He reached in, pulling out the only soggy looking Quetzal bill in there.

"I didn't make it to the bank today to get more money. I'm sorry, can you cover the rest?" He smiled sheepishly, "I'll make it up to you."

I tossed several extra bills on the table and we got up to leave.

That was an honest mistake. After all, it is rather inconvenient to deal with the banks. They don't seem to stick to their hours and sometimes the lines snake out the door.

I let it slide.

Several days later, Doug and I were out until almost nine at night. Guatemala still smelled of civil war, and soldiers roamed the streets. Everyone was home by dark. We were the only fools still out. We were making our way home and came to a fork in the road. One direction led toward where I live. The other branch in the road, toward where Doug lived. Doug stopped, reached for my hand, he pulled me toward him to kiss me goodnight.

Confused, "Aren't you walking me home?"

"No, I've got to get home by nine or my house mother will be mad at me," he explained. "I don't want to upset her."

"You expect me to walk home by myself?" He could see I was getting mad and made a joke.

"You'll be fine. Besides," looking up and down both streets, "there is no one out here."

"Seriously, you're worried about making her mad! Aren't you a little old for that?" I waited for a change of mind. "Aren't you worried about what could happen to me?"

"You'll be fine," he said as he walked away.

"I hope so."

I marched home with my eyes and ears on hyper-alert, cursing at him and calling him a mama's boy the whole time.

If I had been honest with myself, I could have admitted that I knew what type of person Doug was from the get-go. But I let the nagging voice rumble on, convincing myself the voice was nothing at all.

Not long after that he moved into Doña Olga's house. I didn't know until one day I got home from the school and there he was, in the room directly across from me. I got a lecture from the school administration that we couldn't be fraternizing in her house. I explained nothing was going on. But they didn't believe me.

I didn't like this control and neither did Doug. We found a house and moved in with an American guy, a Swiss girl and one of the Guatemalan teachers.

We spent a lot more time together after that. He accompanied me on my school trips. On my weekends off, we adventured through Guatemala and Central America. Our relationship became serious.

Sometime in early fall, his sixteen-year-old sister was in all sorts of teenage trouble. His mom thought he could help her, since neither of the parents were having an effect. Doug's mother wanted Doug to return to New Mexico. And so he did.

About six weeks or so later, Doug invited me to move to Santa Fe to be with him. I missed him terribly. I booked my flight to New Mexico.

chapter seven

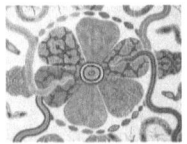

A seagull calls, drawing me back to the island.
With a sting, the breeze salts my sunbaked lips. I lick them, gulping down the memory.

It's late, and Doug still hasn't returned. *Oh well,* I might as well maximize my beach time.

I enter the warm Indian Ocean for a final dip, dropping my clothes on the white powdery beach.

I take my sadness with me and let it sink into the ocean with the setting sun. While floating on my back, I notice hundreds of giant fruit bats fly across the darkening sky. I close my eyes, losing myself in the splash of rain droplets pouring from the heavens.

I think I hear my name being called.

"Georgina!" through waterlogged ears.

How can that be?

Curious, I push my legs downwards until I'm treading water. I squint at the shore line as rain drops bounce off the salty surface up into my eyes. I see a blurred white smile and dreadlocks. I know exactly who it is.

My pulse quickens as the thoughts of his captivating smile dances in my mind and I say to myself, *"If this is supposed to mean something give me a real, unmistakable sign."*

By now, he's already knee high in water, shouting through the pounding rain, "Can I swim with you?"

Before I can answer, he encircles me. Eye pleading, he asks again, "Will you have dinner with me?"

I put on my best tough-girl act, and in a stern voice say, "No, I'm married, I told you," but wishing I wasn't.

The rain begins to let up a little. I swim to the shoreline, with Sunley's wet mop floating in my wake. On shore, I reach for my sarong.

"Why are you making me so sad, Georgina?"

I laugh, wrapping the hibiscus-flowered sarong around my wet curves. I continue to play the cold-shoulder game and walk toward the hotel entrance when I hear him shout:

"I'll be waiting for you with my cocos." His arms wave wildly, pointing down the beach where I see a pyramid of precisely stacked coconuts.

I smile at his boyishness. Daydreaming about his mocha skin glistening with rain drops, I nearly crash into Doug.

"Oh, hey. Did you just get back from work?" I ask. My pulse races. I take a big breath to keep my voice even while trying to remain nonchalant.

"Sorry I'm late. Let's go for a walk on the beach," he suggests. We walk through the hotel gate. Sunley and three other money changers lean with crossed ankles against a sprawling tree limb. They wait for hotel guests who are looking for better than the government's set exchange rate. Our eyes lock for less than a breath. Pretending I don't see him, I turn away.

"Hello, Georgina," he calls out icily.

Rejection rifles from his eyes and leaves shrapnel in my heart.

I cringe.

I feel annoyed. Seriously! Just because we talked he has the right to act jealous, especially since he knows I'm married?

We cross the warm, white sand. Doug untucks his work shirt, the bottom edges flap like laundry in the breeze.

A short distance along the beach, Doug asks, "Who was the Stephen Marley guy?"

"Who?" I play dumb.

"The good-looking guy with the dreads."

"A money changer I met on the beach," I attempt to say with indifference.

I continue, hoping to appeal to Doug's spend-thriftiness. "If you exchange your money with one of these black-market guys you will get ten Seychellois Rupees to one of our dollars." Doug looks interested. "And if you change your money at the bank, you only get three Rupees."

"That's quite a big difference. I can see why they are hanging out by the hotel." Doug nods in response.

I quickly run out of things to say.

Doug picks up the conversation and in a flat drone and tells me about his work day. I watch the water flirt with the sand. It dares to soak his khaki pants rolled up below his knees before retreating into the Indian Ocean.

Twilight throws a black robe across the water. And, Doug's voice lulls me, transporting me to earlier in the day.

Back to the sunshine glinting in Sunley's amber-flecked eyes.

chapter eight

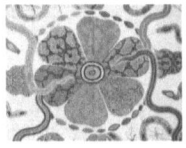

The next morning in the buffet line, Doug looks at me oddly.

"Have you ever been attracted to someone besides me?" His freckles turn burnt orange.

Odd question, what's he really saying? Is he talking about Pria? Or is he referring to Sunley?

"I notice you can't keep your eyes off Pria," I say reactively. "You stare at her and ignore me completely."

It's never the two of us eating dinner together.

Pria, from Mauritius, with liquid dark eyes is here alone.

Doug always invites her to join us.

I feel rude saying no. After all, she is very nice. But they carry on with work-related conversation like I'm not even there. It's not so much the conversation but more how Doug looks intently into her eyes.

This isn't the first time I have been invisible to Doug. I used to think it was me being insecure. That niggling sensation I get in the pit of my belly when he's having a sexually energetic connection with another woman. I couldn't explain it or give "proof." I would tell myself it was just in my imagination.

But I had proof once.

A Guatemalan friend of ours we knew from our time in Guatemala, then she was only fifteen. About ten years later she stayed at our house for a few days. I came home from work one day, and I saw her sitting on Doug's lap. They were laughing.

I glared. Put my hands on my hips and she dismounted, like nothing was going on.

After that, I knew that niggling wasn't my imagination.

My attention drifts back to breakfast, replaying the conversation in my head.

"I am not attracted to her," he says defending himself. "We work together." Then he adds, trying to make her seem less intriguing, "and she is very intelligent."

We sit down at an empty table.

The waitstaff fills our cups with robust African coffee. I close my eyes a second, as the aroma wafts up and fills my senses with pleasure. Feeling more in my body, I look him squarely in the eyes.

He turns his gaze onto the food on his plate.

"I met someone on the beach who has asked me to dinner. I keep saying no and tell him I'm married."

Just then Pria glides like a swan through still water over to our table. Doug leaps up to leave, giving me a stiff-lipped kiss good-bye, trailing in the wake of her exotic beauty.

Deserted, I sit at the table messy with napkins, dirty plates and silverware a while longer, wondering what to do.

I decide to go for a swim and work on my tan. I look like a ghost compared to those Europeans.

It takes less than an hour to burn my alabaster skin before I retreat under the amazing tree whose limbs reach out to embrace me within its shade.

I'm not really relaxing and enjoying lying on the beach at all. My insides churn the entire time, debating whether to meander down the beach in Sunley's direction. If I walk only a short way down the beach, I reason, I should be able to spot Sunley from the shoreline just outside of the hotel property. That is, if he is working.

After about thirty seconds of walking, I see him out of the corner of my eye.

Damn!

I pretend not to notice him while casually continuing with my walk.

"Georgina!" Sunley shouts, sprinting across the sand.

I stop and let him catch up. I look down at my feet and circle my big toe in the sugary white sand. My heart races with excitement. I don't know what to say. Luckily, Sunley breaks the awkward silence.

He points to the shade under one of the elegant swaying palms to a neatly stacked pyramid of coconuts. "Would you like a coconut?" I hang on every word as his alluring creole accent pulls me towards him.

We walk up the incline of the beach, both looking at each other with silly grins.

Not saying a word.

He points to a fallen palm, inviting me to sit on its elongated trunk.

Carefully he selects a coconut and hacks off the top's coarse hair. He pries it off with his machete and inserts a flimsy plastic straw. Leaning towards me, he offers me his gift. I giggle like a school girl. *What has come over me? I must be losing my senses.*

I feel the curly hair of his leg brush me as he sits down.

Like magnets, his eyes draw me closer.

The tension is too much.

Heat rises in my body that makes my palms perspire. I convince myself it is just the humidity. I'm trying hard to resist him, but he is wearing down my resolve.

chapter nine

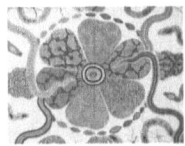

I can't wait for my daily visits with Sunley.

I haven't felt this excited and alive in so long.

With each step that draws me closer to his coconut stand, the caged parrot in my belly flaps her wings ferociously.

Black granite boulders, considered the hardest and oldest in the world, guard secluded aquamarine tide pools. We hide amongst the protective monoliths, our backs soften against the warm stone, melting shoulder to shoulder. Sinfully, we hold hands, searching out the lines of our destiny.

I hide my clandestine daily excursions with Sunley from Doug. I don't know if "hide" is the right word. I just never talk about that part of my day, and Doug never thinks to ask, but I make up my mind to take Sunley up on his invitation to dinner.

"I decided I want to go to dinner with that Stephen Marley guy," I announce one afternoon.

I expect Doug to launch into a tirade of objection. Perhaps I was hoping he would become insanely possessive, realizing I was slipping away.

But nothing.

No reaction. Only, "When will you be going?"

In the meantime, Doug arranges to meet Pria.

That evening, as I blow-dry my hair and put on lip gloss, Doug asks, "Where are you guys going?"

"I'm not sure. I'm meeting him around six when he's finished work and then we're going out somewhere. I won't be too long."

Curious, "Where are you going with Pria?"

"Just for pizza and a drink down the road," he says, now sitting in the other room.

I'm seething inside as I dab with my pinky finger the skin between the arch in my lips where the lip gloss escaped. It's more than odd to me that he seems fine with me going out with another man.

He's not even trying to stop me. I wish for one last moment, he'd claim me, implore me not to go. But no, not a hint of jealousy or questioning why I want to go.

He doesn't care. As if he wants me gone.

My heart aches, again.

"See you later," I say, competing with the noise coming from the TV.

I walk out the door.

I feel detached and numb. That feeling you get when your feet fall asleep, but it's all over, inside and out. But I put on a smile as I approach Sunley's speckled rusty and navy Toyota pick-up truck.

"I was so worried you wouldn't come. I have been waiting patiently for you, hanging out with my friends." He gestures at a group of bare-chested muscly men in swimming trunks. They acknowledge me, tipping their heads with polite nods.

With a light bounce in his barefoot step, Sunley walks around to what would be the driver's side at home and opens the door for me.

Thanking him, I climb in and sit down on torn, sun-bleached fabric. I notice his broad toes and clean toenails against the clutch and how they expand across the pedal as he changes gears as we drive the curvy road into town.

I don't know if I should be doing this. The pit of my stomach wrenches tight.

I hear him ask, "Beaut-ee-ful, what would you like to eat?"

I relax. Flattered, I smile and say, "Anything is fine." I'm lost in the compliment and his Seychellois accent.

He stops near the movie theater in Victoria. He hops out and dashes into a small restaurant. From the truck window, I can see grease pooling atop the pepperoni pizza on display under a heat lamp. He orders four medium-sized square pieces of pizza.

Jumping back into the truck, "I want to take you to my house. It's not so far from here."

"Okay."

"But I want to pick up some beer before I take you there."

Am I crazy?

A cocktail of excitement and fear stirs. *I don't know him, really. Doug doesn't know where I am or how to find me.* "I'll be fine." My inner voice soothes me.

One more stop at a small grocery store. Sunley returns with a pack of SeyBrew Lager and passes the cans over to me.

The road ribbons and winds until we are somewhere on the opposite side of the hills from my hotel. And, the other side of town.

Matchbox-size houses, mainly constructed from cinder block and corrugated tin, tightly squeezed onto stamp-size plots of land. Where he lives with his mother is no different.

We park on the side of the house, and I follow Sunley underneath a corrugated tin roof, covering the outside toilet, shower and kitchen area.

"This is the toilet," Sunley says, pointing to the left as we walk past the white lidless porcelain bowl. Continuing, we pass the shower and the kitchen, which are separate from the main part of the house. There is a small walkway opening into a room with a narrow white fridge and two wooden chairs tucked under a small plastic table.

I hear the sound of a muffled newscast somewhere in the belly of the house.

"My mom is here. I will introduce you. But she only speaks Creole and French." he warns.

Sunley makes his way across the dark brown tile with pink roses on them. He takes the SeyBrew from my hands and puts them in the fridge. And puts the pizza on a small table flush with the wall.

I follow him down an unlit narrow hallway. He stops in front of a door on our right and with a key from his keychain, he unlocks the brass padlock and quickly flips the shackle to the side.

He leads me further down the hallway past a room exploding with clothes into the living room.

A short, curly-white-haired woman in her seventies with freckles on her cafe-latte skin sits on the far end of the sofa listening to the radio. She ignores us until Sunley says, "Ma-ma." Without a smile, eyes painted with disdain look up at me.

Smiling at her, "Bonjour," I say, remembering some French I learned from my school days. I must have made a bad impression. She immediately leaves her radio show and goes into her room.

I feel awkward, sure that she doesn't like me.

Sunley turns off the radio.

"Please sit." He invites courteously, gesturing toward the floral sofa.

I choose a location on the sofa far enough away from him, so we don't touch. He turns toward me and passes me a slice of square pizza. I devour it hungrily. He offers me the second piece, laughing. "Doesn't your husband feed you?"

"Funny! Lunch was a long time ago."

After a few more bites I'm done.

"Excuse me," I get up off the stiff sofa, "I'll be right back." I walk down the hallway, past his mom's room with light seeping under the door and locate the outside bathroom.

Re-entering the living room, my eyes widen.

Sunley reclines against the sofa. The black circular centers of his amber eyes elongate into an ellipse, penetrating mine.

Distracted by movement, I break his gaze and look down.

His right hand encircles his rather small but erect ebony penis. Moving his hand rhythmically up and down the shaft, he asks, "Do you want to suck my cock?"

My eyes bug out. My teeth clench, which gives me a shooting pain up into my right temple.

What?

Mortified and humiliated, I shout, "I am not your whore! Take me home right now!"

And with that, I stomp out of the house and wait outside next to his jalopy of a truck. On the drive back, I say nothing but stew in disgust and confusion. *Did I really give off that image? Who does he think I am?*

He drops me off at the fancy, flowery entrance to my expensive hotel.

"Good-bye, Georgina," he says in a quiet voice.

"Bye," I respond gruffly and slam the door as I jump off the torn seat.

Maybe he's the one that feels like a whore, I suddenly think. Immediately, I feel guilty. He did tell me about some of the women he met here, that had stayed in this hotel. He told me many of them just want an exotic vacation and that means sex with an exotic man, too.

I don't put myself in that same class of women. I'm not looking for an exotic man on my island vacation. But if I am really honest with myself I am looking for ... something different.

I just didn't know it would be packaged this way.

chapter ten

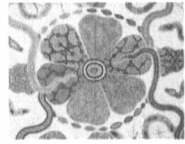

I see the light shining out of our window on the second floor. It's not late, and Doug is already back.

"You're back already? How was dinner?"

"Not very good. We just had street pizza," I say flatly. I am still stinging from the humiliation.

I tell Doug what happened.

Infuriated, he says, "That pig! You're lucky he didn't try to rape you. What were you thinking?"

"He didn't seem like that at all. He was fun, and we laughed a lot. I thought he was a nice guy." I still think he's a nice guy, something went wrong, that's all. Embarrassed enough, I switch topics.

"Where did you and Pria go? You're back pretty early."

"I met her down the road. She thought you were coming, too, and that's why she came. I think she felt uncomfortable, so we had a quick drink and then she left."

I guess he forgot to mention that I wouldn't be there.

The next day, we leave the little island of Mahé and fly farther south across the blue-jewel expanse of the Indian Ocean. We land in Mauritius and take a forty-five-minute cab ride past fields of tall knife-shaped leaves of sugar cane, arriving in Flic en Flac on the western part of the island.

We arrive at our hotel and walk through the airy lobby. Tall tropical plants boasting bright orange and scarlet blooms usher us toward the front desk. A young man of East Indian descent in his mid-twenties, wearing a grey and burgundy uniform, gives us our key while carefully explaining where the stairs are that will lead up to our room.

As we continue through the lobby past several wicker chairs with cream cushions, I ask Doug, "Why do they always put us in such luxurious hotels? Not that I'm complaining."

"They are afraid for our safety mostly and that we wouldn't be comfortable in anything that isn't up to American standards. They don't know how we have traveled and the places we have slept."

"If they did, they might be really shocked. Remember in Guatemala when we slept outside next to that old shack, and in the morning, we were covered with flea bites! Or when we slept on a picnic table for a weekend!" I laugh. "We didn't think anything of it. That was part of the fun."

He looks down at me, the outside corners of his eyes crinkling, "Yeah, we did some crazy trips!" He smiles.

This hotel is much bigger than our hotel in the Seychelles. We walk past an outside bar perched between the pool and the beach. With the sun beginning to slump over the horizon, the water appears a melancholy slate.

After crossing the nearly football-sized field of carefully mown grass, we climb the stairs to the second floor and walk down the corridor to our room. Entering the room, I see the crisp white linens on the king-sized bed, a desk and a couple of cushy chairs. My eyes follow the contents of the room and linger a moment on the dark brown linen curtains gently waving in the breeze whispering through the open window. I walk over, casting my eyes past the manicured grounds until they find the sea. A wave of sadness overcomes me, my heart tightening. I brush it away. "Isn't this a beautiful room?"

"Yes. It's a really large room."

"Do you want to go to the bar and get a drink?" he invites me.

I push the unexplainable sadness into a back corner of my heart.

"Let me put on my swimsuit first. Maybe we could go for a swim. It's nearly six, but there is probably some daylight left."

We find a couple of reclining wooden lounging chairs and put our feet up. The waiter, dressed in a virgin-white uniform, carefully balancing a tray of empty glasses, approaches us.

Our drinks arrive, and the alcohol seeps slowly into my blood. My body begins to relax, and my breath deepens. After a while, I walk into the water. *Brr.* It's cold! I let out a shriek as Doug laughs and gets off the lounger to join me. He takes my hand, and we wade out deeper into the water. When the water gets just about my neck height, I start bobbing on my toes. He circles his arm around my waist and pulls me to him. I'm suddenly nervous by this unexpected display of affection. I don't really know how to react. My body stiffens as he squeezes me tighter. Doug notices the tension and releases me.

I dive beneath the murky surface. Swimming underwater, I pop up several yards away. Doug swims after me playfully.

"I'm going to catch you!"

"I don't think so, I'm a fast swimmer." I taunt him and slip out of his reach.

When he almost touches my ankle, I flip around and grab his hand and tote him toward the shore.

The sun takes a quick sip of ocean before it dips below the horizon and into the underworld for the night.

The air temperature drops quickly. "I'm getting cold. Do you want to go and get ready for dinner?"

Dinner is packed with families with English accents and honeymoon couples. Tiki torches light up the beach, and we select a table that holds eight people. The other six are from the same family. The dinner is buffet style. The father asks Doug what he does, and everyone seems fascinated by his work and the trips we have been on. I'm noticing that feeling of invisibility when a plump blonde woman in her early fifties asks me what I do. I hate that question. But I respond, "I'm a massage therapist."

"Oh. That must be hard work."

"It can be. But I am pretty strong."

She smiles politely and looks toward Doug and her husband, who are still talking.

I'm uncomfortable with all this small talk. I get lost in the thought, *what went wrong with Sunley?* We were having so much fun. Then he got weird. Really weird.

I'm still pondering the question when Doug interrupts my closed-loop thinking.

"Are you ready to go back to the room?" He notices I'm off in la-la land.

"Yeah, let's go." I quickly get up. "It was nice to meet you," I courteously tell the woman and her family as I tuck my chair under the white polyester tablecloth dangling over the edge.

Back in our room I plop down on the soft cotton comforter and start writing in my journal. Doug turns on the TV and locates the local news.

I muse over the journey here and the day's events. I hate that I'm comparing everything here to the Seychelles. Maybe because everything is small and cute in the Seychelles, everything here seems a bit uninteresting and blah. I notice how I am obsessing over my unknowable question about Sunley. In one breath, I am mortified and disgusted. The next, I want to solve the problem and make it right. I'm not even on this island, Mauritius. I am still back on Mahé.

I put my journal on the grey marble night stand to my right and reach up to turn off the light. Doug sees me readying for sleep, and he turns off the TV.

Then he leans over and plants his lips on mine. I dutifully return the kiss as my body curls inward, closing him out. But this appears as an invitation, and he crawls on top of me. He brings his mouth toward mine, attempting another kiss. I smile and push firmly on his upper chest.

"I'm sorry, Doug. I'm really tired from the travel."

He wiggles off me, lying there, barely breathing. I say nothing to ease his discomfort, and after another minute he leans over to his side of the bed and clicks off the light.

"Good-night," he says.

"Good-night."

I stare at the ceiling, not really tired. I'm shrouded in mental torment.

Doug's snoring amps up. I dig out a pair of spongey orange ears plugs and squish them into my ears.

chapter eleven

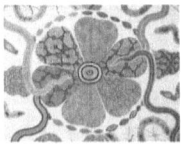

Doug's ride arrives by seven forty-five in the morning, and he takes off for his workshop in Port Louis.

I decide it's time for breakfast and make my way to the restaurant. The dark beams hold up the thatched structure in a teepee shape. A waiter ushers me to a table overlooking the grass. He deftly removes the napkin, and with a graceful swoop, it softly lands like falling snow across my lap.

Smiling with delight, I say, "Thank you!" This luxurious treatment amuses me, mostly from being unaccustomed to receiving the finer things in life and maybe, receiving in general.

He quickly flips over the white china coffee cup, offering me tea or coffee. Coffee, of course.

I'm impressed with the buffet's abundance and select a variety of fresh fruit, yogurt, eggs, and fried potatoes. I take my time eating as I have nowhere to be.

I try to read my crinkled copy of *Blue Horizon* by Wilbur Smith, but I can't concentrate. I replay, again, the events with Sunley. And, again, asking that same useless question, What happened? I don't understand. Over and over again.

Enough already! I reprimand myself.

I've got to do something to distract myself.

The open ceiling feels like it is crushing me.

I beckon the waiter and ask him to bring me the check. I rapidly scrawl my name and write our room number.

Up in the room, I wriggle into my swimsuit. I look out the window across immaculate grounds, and an apple-shaped tree catches my eye. This is a perfect place to write in my journal and read. I put it in my pack along with a towel and some sunscreen.

I go for a swim in the stormy-grey water. I sit in one of the hotel's lounge chairs drawing hearts with my toes. The golden sand feels much coarser on my feet. I can't relax. I'm restless. I get out my iPod and listen to Swahili lesson number five.

"I understand a little," says the recorded male African voice.

Mimi nafuhamu kidogo. I respond in a whisper, so no one overhears me.

"Now say, 'I understand a little.'"

Nana sema kidogo.

His bass-drum voice begins to hypnotize me.

"Listen and say in Swahili, 'I don't speak very well.'"

Si sema ... The image of Sunley squatting in front of me. His dazzling gold-flecked amber eyes tease me.

Damn it!

I'm lagging two sentences behind in my lesson.

Apparently not paying attention anymore, I turn off my iPod.

The following couple of days follow a similar routine.

My mind is wound so tightly.

At night, when Doug and I are in bed he wrangles me under him, locking his lips onto mine, pressing his body close to me.

Why is he behaving amorously now? He hasn't paid attention to me in ages.

I feel wrenched apart by guilt. My mind obsesses over someone else. My heart hurts like hunger pangs.

I let him have his way with me, and I fly away to the top of the nearby volcano. Only to return when I feel the rumbling snores vibrate the bed.

Tears leak from my eyes.

And I turn my back to him as they slide over the bridge of my nose onto the bleach-perfumed white sheets.

chapter twelve

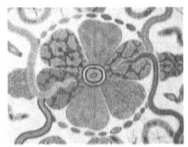

We spend our last afternoon and evening in Port Louis at a hotel arranged for us by the State Department.

I notice a flock of flight attendants ascending the transparent glass elevator and a few European-looking businessmen at the bar.

Doug and I wander through the city. Mauritius is multicultural with people from India, Africa, China, and a few European countries. There is no official language and no official religion. We walk down a street decorated with silks, baskets of fragrant spices and pashmina scarves. I stop at an open kiosk and select a soft pink and baby blue scarf, caressing it and holding it to my cheek. I decide this is the one. I pay for it, and we continue down the street. As we wander, we notice a hill with a domed building.

"Do you want to climb the hill and see what is up there?" Doug asks.

"Yeah, that sounds like fun."

"Let's find out how to get up there."

We continue walking down streets past private schools and precisely painted houses until we are near the base of the hill. Doug asks an elderly man walking with a cane how to get to the top. He points a bit to the right, explaining where the road to the top begins.

Eventually, we find it. Walking up the snaking, narrow road, we pass a couple of people on their way down. I pause to catch my breath and turn around, looking out across the tops of the whitewashed stone buildings. It doesn't take long before we are on top of the hill, where a large sign indicates we've arrived at Citadel Fort Adelaide. We walk through grass, viewing the entire city. Slightly panting and sweating heavily, I inhale deeply, smelling the salt water wafting on the breeze. My thoughts jump back to the Seychelles, to Sunley.

I look over at Doug. He's quiet, lost in his thoughts. He looks over at me. I smile, mostly to mask what my eyes might reveal.

We walk around the stone fort before we make the quick jaunt back to the city. On our way back to the hotel, we stop in at a store selling silk clothing. I try on a couple of daringly sexy tops that look like tuxedo vests with a corset back and a plunging V in the front. I select the icy blue and the scarlet red.

Later that night, Doug suggests we have a drink at the hotel's bar. I put on my new icy blue top. I'm not feeling bold enough to wear red, just yet. Doug brings his laptop and sets it up at the bar, answering emails. I finish my beer. He's still on his computer. I move next to him. He's staring at the screen. I move even closer and press my boobs against his right arm. He glances in my direction, then resumes his work.

Annoyed, I get up and find a more comfortable chair in the lounge area.

I can't believe he's not paying attention to me! I think I look pretty hot.

I ruminate on how much attention Sunley paid to me. How often he called me, bee-u-te-ful Georgina. Playing the words in my ears like a song, I start to feel better about myself and angrier at Doug.

After what seems a long time, Doug looks up from his laptop and scans the lounge for me. He closes the black plastic cover and puts it in his backpack before he makes his way to me. "Do you want to go somewhere for a drink?"

I scowl at him through cat-slit eyes. "I suppose."

"Let me put this up in the room first," he says, tapping the side of his backpack.

I rise from my seat and follow him to the escalator. Once in our room, I go to the bathroom and check myself in the mirror. Maybe I don't look as good as I thought. Perhaps that's the problem. I make a half turn and catch the blue silk strings holding my top together. Then the other direction. Leaning closer, I reapply clear lip gloss. I stand back to get a complete look. No, I look pretty good, I decide.

We cross over a couple of streets and spot a patio with some people outside sipping from tall glasses with mint sprigs floating amongst the ice cubes. We find two chairs and sit. I order one of those rum-filled fancy mint drinks and Doug orders a beer.

"Are you excited about going back to the Seychelles? I won't have work to do this time around. So, we can go diving and snorkeling and check out some of the other islands." He pauses and tips his beer back.

"That sounds like fun." Without conviction. "We can play it by ear. We have a whole week."

"Yeah, I know. But it will go fast, and if we don't plan anything the time will go by, and we won't have done anything except sit on the beach."

"That sounds good to me!" I could do that every day.

"I was reading about some of the other islands. There is one called La Digue. It's supposed to be romantic, a honeymooner's island, they call it in the guidebook."

"Okay." But, I notice pressure building and my stomach tightening at the thought. "Good." He smiles at me. "My guidebook says the boats over there only leave in the morning." He's thinking aloud. "We are going to have to spend a night on Mahé, since we arrive in the afternoon."

chapter thirteen

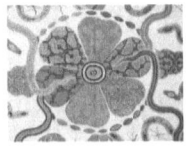

We arrive at the Seychelles airport and search out the car-rental booth.

They give us a small crimson Ford Fiesta with plenty of room to throw our backpacks in the trunk. Doug drives cautiously since he isn't used to driving on the wrong side of the road. I feel the tension but keep my mouth shut. Until we reach the round-about.

He takes the inside lane. I hope he knows what he's doing!

Gripping the seat. "Do you know how to drive around these?"

"It can't be that hard," he says with gravelly irritation.

I grip the seat harder until we have clearly made it through the gauntlet of cars, which appear to be randomly exiting this way and that. Finally, we are back on the road leading to the part of the island where we stayed before.

The black granite rocks loom at the edge of the road as we approach the final curve.

"Let's check this place out first and see how much it is," he says as he makes a quick exit off the road and stops before a brick house with peeling mango-colored paint and a sign that says, "Georgina's Cottage Beach Guest House."

"That's cool. It has my name!" I laugh.

We enter through the small gate, leading into an entryway and office area. Extending from here is the dining area for breakfast and beyond that the kitchen.

Doug inquires how much. We already had an idea from his guidebook. This was the least expensive place listed on the island, and it is still fifty dollars! We fill out the required guest information and include our passport numbers. The man attending us reads it over to ensure we filled it out correctly.

"Your name is Georgina?" he asks in surprise.

"Yes. I've never had anything named after me before," I joke.

"That was my mother's name," he says tenderly.

"It's a good name." I smile at him.

"Here are your keys." Doug takes them. "Your room is around the front in the middle."

"Oh, and breakfast starts at seven and finishes by nine."

"Okay. Thanks."

We unlock the door of our room and enter. I walk past a low bed with a brown and yellow cover. The bathroom contains a shower with a pale pink, plastic shower curtain. Simple. I go to the bed and plonk on it. The thin mattress responds with squeaky springs. I bounce a minute.

"Well, I guess I got spoiled with those fancy hotels," I laugh. "No worries, I'll survive."

"You are spoiled."

This will be only five days before we are fly to Zanzibar. And, probably another luxury hotel.

We take our bags out of the trunk and set them on the wooden slat table. I change into my navy-blue tankini. The click of our flip-flops sounds as we walk down the road. When the sandy part of the beach begins we cross the road to walk in the sand. We walk down the beach until we arrive at a little outdoor bar under a palm-thatched palapa.

We order a couple of SeyBrews and sit on some wobbly high-legged wooden stools.

Doug is talking to me, but I am far away. Well, actually just down the beach, thinking of Sunley. And pondering the eternal problem of what went wrong until I've worked my brain and my stomach into a knotted nervous mess. I can't sit here anymore.

"Doug. I know this is crazy, but I want to talk to Sunley," I blurt impulsively.

His jaw drops and his eyelids peel back, "Seriously, after what happened? You're crazy." Shaking his head, he swivels away from me.

"I know. But I won't have any peace until I understand what happened." The memory stings, slapping me again. I lower my head in humiliation.

He rolls his eyes and takes a swig of beer.

"I won't be long. An hour tops," I promise.

"Wait for me here." I jump off the stool, "I'll see you soon!"

And I walk out of the bar.

chapter fourteen

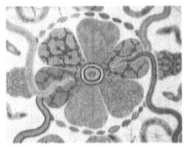

The hot sand flicks up onto my feet, momentarily distracting me from the rope twisting ever tighter in my belly.

Shit. I tell myself. *What have I done?*

Half hoping he won't be on the beach, I continue walking in the direction of where Sunley keeps his coconuts.

He isn't here. I look into the coconut palms, and I still don't see him.

Whew, exhaling with relief.

But then another impulse overrules my logical mind.

"Excuse me," I say to a woman wearing a red plaid shirt and selling shell jewelry, "Do you know where Sunley might be?"

She points down the beach toward the direction I've just come from.

"Thank you."

I could just keep going back to the bar. I don't have to do this.

On my right near the life guard stand, I see the back of his dreads. He is with two other guys, talking closely in a tight circle.

Keep walking. Just keep going.

But ... no.

I march up toward the men and stop about three feet away. They break the circle. Sunley is standing alone.

I hope he can't see my pounding heart through my swim suit.

"Sunley." I beckon him over with my hand.

He moves closer to me.

But something about his eyes aren't quite right.

They seem vacant. As if his soul has flown from his body. There is not even a fleeting recognition of me.

How stupid of me. He is as he appeared to be.

"Who are you?" he asks, truly not remembering me.

My shoulders curl in, protecting my heart. I feel deflated.

"I'm going." I turn to leave.

Grabbing my arm, "No, wait. Your name will come to me." He looks up to the right and then gives me a charming smile.

"Is it Patricia?"

"No," I say gruffly, crossing my arms in front of my chest. I take a step away from him.

Following at my heels, "Is it Maria?"

"No." I take another step.

"Let's sit here." Pointing to the sand. "I will remember. Give me time."

Still standing with arms crossed.

I turn away from him toward the bar where I left Doug.

He grabs my arms. I stop and turn toward the sea. He lists a few more names.

"Stay until I remember." Each name becomes part of the riddle.

Now it has become a game.

Tired of standing, I plop onto the sand. Sunley lowers himself gracefully down into a lotus position next to me.

He's quiet a moment, conjuring more names from his memory bank.

Staring straight ahead over the vast cobalt ocean.

I'm wounded.

My name should have come to him automatically. It's only been five days. And "Georgina" is a common name in Africa. Besides there is a B & B that he drives by every day to get here.

Reaching over to me, he pats my abdomen, "Is it my baby?"

"No!"

Great! Now he thinks I'm fat.

Estimating the time, I'm guessing I've been gone about half an hour. I adjust my legs under me. Leaning forward, I push up with my hands, ready to walk away.

Suddenly, like an exuberant child Sunley bursts out, "Georgina, Georgina, Georgina!" He laughs excitely, solving the riddle. "I remembered."

My eyes bore into his. The vacancy now filling with light, brightening each time he repeats my name.

That was weird. He was gone. Now he is back.

He sidles closer to me. "I didn't think you would come back," he says timidly like an abandoned child. My heart softens, he's feeling more like the person I knew before.

Then he says, "Business is slow. Let's go get something to eat."

chapter fifteen

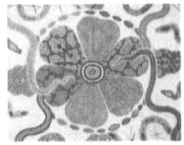

I'm torn.
I feel guilty about not telling Doug where I'm going. Especially since I told him I'd only be gone an hour at the most. But I feel righteously selfish, leaving in Sunley's truck we drive to the other side of the island.

I follow Sunley through the open breezeway and into the house.

"Do you want to take a shower?" he asks.

Does he mean by myself or together?

"I'll cook dinner for you, and you can shower while you wait for me."

"Okay." I sigh in relief. "I've got sand in my swimsuit."

"I will get you a towel." He spins on his heel, heading towards his bedroom.

I shift from one foot to the other, waiting for his return. "Thank you," I respond as he passes me a slightly crunchy sun-dried towel. I make my way to the shower.

Copper pipes run horizontally across the tin wall, branching up to the shower head. Heat radiates from the hot, tin roof, pouring down like an invisible sun eliminating the need for hot water. Turning on the tap, I close my eyes. I let lukewarm water wash away the sand, along with my conscience.

Curry spices waft over the corrugated tin wall. My belly rumbles in anticipation of Sunley's cooking.

I wrap the towel around me, tucking the corner tightly and securing it in place underneath my armpits. I walk four footsteps and peer around the corner into the kitchen. I watch him flip the fish onto its other side. Sunley looks up from his cooking, "Do you want to borrow my t-shirt and shorts?" I had only brought what I had on, my swimsuit.

"Yes, please." He sets the fork to the rocking, warped frying pan and trots off down the hallway.

I follow him into his room. He opens the mahogany wooden doors of a standup wardrobe. From his sparse collection of hanging clothes, he yanks a t-shirt off a hanger and grabs a pair of shorts from a shelf.

"My fish!" he shrieks before dashing back into the kitchen.

I put on the camouflaged grey and black shirt and the navy-blue nylon shorts. I smile at the slightly too-big feel of Sunley's clothes loosely hugging my body.

I find him in the dimly lit kitchen. The only light comes from the open doorway and a greasy lightbulb dangling from an electric cord. I glance at the space, noticing he only has a couple of forks with bent tines, a handful of spoons, and chipped plates.

My privileged-guilt impulsively wants to give him something. I want to buy him a knife set, like the fancy German set I have at home. He only has one knife, so well worn it bows like a canoe.

My heart flutters and spreads warm honey across my chest. Sunley looks up at me and gives me a toothy grin. I smile and lower my eyes, not wanting to reveal myself.

He has so little compared to me. I have so much I don't even appreciate.

Finishing at the stove, he scoops half onto a plate and serves me with a smile.

"Let's sit in there." He points across the breezeway to the main part of the house.

Sitting down, I take a bite.

"You're a pretty good cook," I tell him, enjoying the creamy coconut curried flavors.

We talk easily, laughing a lot at each other. But I'm counting the grains of rice left on my plate, watching them disappear, one by one. He sits patiently until I'm finished. He springs to his feet and gathers the plates.

On his return, he picks up my hand and leads me down the hallway toward the bedroom.

I hesitate, sticking my feet like Velcro to the brown and pink rose tile.

Shit, I should get back to Doug. He's been waiting a long time.

But I ignore that voice, and I follow his bouncing palm tree of dreads to his room.

Getting a better look this time, I notice he has a small TV, and the sheets on his bed are polka-dotted with the brown curled holes of cigarette burns.

Turning on the fan he asks, "Do you like Lenny Kravitz?"

"Yes."

"I've been told I look like him," he remarks while putting a Lenny Kravitz DVD into the player.

I sit down on the very edge of the bed, looking at him more closely. Then at the man singing on the TV and back and forth a couple of times.

I don't know about that. Other than the roasted coffee-colored hair and dark skin. But I smile anyway.

He has no shame in singing out loud to *"Fly Away"* at the top of his lungs. I laugh, wishing I had that same fearlessness.

The song over, he switches his attention to me, sweeping a renegade blonde hair out of my eyes.

I cast my eyes downward, pretending to look at my tanned knees.

He gently lifts my chin up, so my eyes meet him.

I want to snap my head away, afraid of what he will see but he locks his lips against mine. The taste of curry and cigarettes linger on my taste buds. Now, I'm not running away.

I let him ease me onto the firm mattress until I feel his compact muscled body on me. A sea-salt scented dread bristles on my forehead, I compare the slight weight and famished kiss to Doug's.

Night and day.

Apprehensive, I concentrate on the tight curls of chest hair against my breasts, noticing how pale I am under his ebony skin.

chapter sixteen

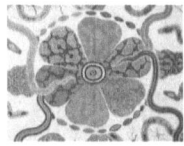

His tongue grazes quickly across the puckering skin surrounding my nipples.

He pops one into his mouth, consuming me like a fresh ripe apricot before he moves ravenously onto the other one. His mouth moves on, and he bites me gently in the valley between my breast.

I exhale as the tension releases.

His tongue roams across my belly. Hands reaching up to pluck at my engorged nipples.

Dragging his fingers across my smooth inner thighs, he spreads my legs apart and pushes my knees into a frog position. He hoists himself onto me; our golden and black curls mingle a moment. He does a half pushup, launching his arrow into the target. I gasp, sucking in air. Holding my breath, he pumps in and out.

Wool and salt cover my nose as his dreads start to feel scratchy against my face.

In a husky voice, "Roll over," he says, rising to his knees.

Obeying, I slowly roll onto my belly. He puts his hands onto the underside of my abdomen. Using my hip bones for handles, he pulls my butt up until it locks like Lego onto his hungry hips. With rapid pulsing motions he thrusts himself mechanically in and out of me. I hear his skin slapping skin. I peak over my shoulder. His eyes closed. He's off in his own world.

I could be anyone.

I don't know what I expected it to feel like. I guess I want exploding passion; to bring out the hidden parts of me I sense would awaken with the right lover. But I feel like I am a prop in a play he is performing. A routine he is rushing to complete. My heart feels weighted by stones of disappointment.

One final deep thrust and, "Ahhh" leaks from his throat, bringing me back into the room. He pulls out, liquid dripping down my right hamstring. He reaches across me to a full ashtray on the nightstand and finds his cigarette pack. He takes one out, tapping the end on the box and lights it with his little Bic lighter. He inhales deeply, looking at the smoke curl as it escapes out the open window.

"Did you like it?" he asks with pleading eyes.

Smiling back, "Yes," I lie.

He doesn't know my body. I console myself, making an excuse to feel better.

I hear Lenny Kravitz singing "Fly Away" in my head.

"I need to take a shower." And we walk out of the bedroom.

I shower. He's outside, lighting another cigarette. The smoke wafts over the tin roof and settles on me like smog.

I smell of soap, yet I don't feel any cleaner. I put on the t-shirt and shorts I borrowed and step into the breezeway. Sunley stamps out his cigarette in the dirt.

"Will you please take me home now?"

"Won't you stay with me? Sleep here with me tonight," he begs.

"No, I have to get back." *I have some explaining to do.*

chapter seventeen

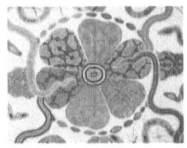

Sunley opens the creaky door of his Toyota. Now it's nearly two in the morning.

I hop in, clutching my damp swimsuit in one hand.

The light beams bend against the trees skirting the narrow road before leaping out in front again, guiding us upon the serpent-twining road. The smell of sea air flying through the open window caresses my face, soothing me as the twenty-minute drive to the other side of the island and to Georgina's B & B drags on.

He turns the headlights off the last few yards. The light lingers a moment before diminishing into a pinprick in the darkness. He parks next to the red Fiesta. I get out, closing the door quietly. Sunley accompanies me to the door.

"I will come see you tomorrow," he whispers with a quick kiss.

I walk in the door and tiptoe around to far side of the bed.

I wonder if Doug heard me? He's not snoring. He could be awake, pretending he's asleep.

I bend down and tuck Sunley's clothes in the shadow of my side of the bed. Delicately, I lift the sheet and carefully crawl in, trying not to jiggle the bed. Hugging to the bed's precipice, I try to fall asleep.

A few hours later Doug wakes me up, "Where have you been all night?" he grills me.

I look outside and notice the soft golden light of dawn creep in through the window.

I wouldn't lie to him.

I know there was no gentle way to say it.

So, I just say it.

"I was with Sunley." And quickly add before I change my mind, "I slept with him."

I stare at him.

An unseen force boils beneath the surface of his skin, as a mountain range of emotions emerge across his features, bringing him to life. A yellow-orange blaze flickers in the bottomless pupils of Doug's hazel eyes. And a fire combusts, melting the waxen mask that has covered his face in the years since his mother's death.

Watching.

The lower right corner of his mouth twitches. Color rushes across the broad landscape of his forehead. Big monsoon-sized tears escape the pools collecting in Doug's bottom lids and slowly slide across his tanned, freckled cheeks.

Barely breathing, waiting to see what will emerge in the tempest, the tsunami of emotion thrashes. As the wave slams against me, Doug lets loose his anger.

"I can't believe you slept with him!" he screams. "What were you thinking?"

The rush of energy bursts the constraints of our relationship.

Suddenly I feel buoyant, floating free. A surfer on the waves, I ride the storm out, surrendering to the currents until I'm washed up on the shore.

I feel all the pain and sadness seep out of his heart onto my ruthless lap. I wish it weren't true, what I had done.

The storm spent, Doug abruptly stops. With a penetrating gaze, he looks through my eyes into my soul to give him the answers he seeks.

I offer no words. I see no point in defending or justifying my actions.

Then, he gets up off the bed like he's suddenly become either very old or very heavy. He shoves all his clothes quickly into his backpack.

I watch in helplessness, wanting so badly to take it all back. To smooth everything over with something pretty. So I won't have to feel the pain.

He reaches the door, tears leaking out of his sad eyes.

He turns around, looking me in the eye, "Good-bye," he says lifelessly.

I feel his agony and my own, but all I can say is, "I'm sorry Doug. I am so sorry I hurt you."

He looks at me blankly, not quite believing me. He lifts the hatch and tosses in his backpack. He gets into the rental car. Spitting dirt, he speeds off.

I wish things didn't have to be so broken for him to feel something.

A fine dust of emptiness settles in the room, infiltrating me and filling me up with anxiety.

I realize I am alone.

All alone.

Abandonment's wringing hand tightly grips me by the throat. My mind lashes out, grasping onto any thought that will stop the sands from slipping out from beneath my feet and leaving me naked, drowning in the vast ocean.

I know I will see him in a few days at the airport when we will fly to Zanzibar.

I could go on about Sunley, but that doesn't seem important now.

chapter eighteen

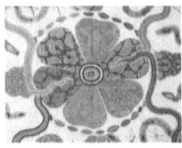

Peering around the X-ray machine at the tiny Mahé airport, I see Doug's auburn head drooped over his laptop like a Raggedy Andy doll.

Nervousness pinches my stomach and leaves a bruise.

I sling my bags across my shoulder and adjust them, stalling, as I wonder what's the best way to approach Doug. I'm wishing I was invisible right now. I walk as if I'm wearing moccasins, hoping the rubber soles of my Keens won't squeak on the polished tiles.

I sit right next to him. He acts like he doesn't know I'm there.

"Hi," I say.

A moment goes by.

He looks up at me, one side of his mouth curls upward. "Hi," he responds and then resumes looking at the laptop screen. I wait another minute wondering what to say. Then pretend everything is normal. "Do you want to talk?" I ask him.

"No."

We board the plane, our seats adjacent. I try to get Doug to talk to me. Mostly, to relieve my own discomfort. By the time we reach Zanzibar, we are making small talk.

Mama Naila greets us, "A-Salama-Alaykum," and warms us with hugs and kisses. It's been two years since we've seen her last.

"I have my car parked in the front," she says.

We follow her out to her forest-green Mitsubishi. A dark-skinned man with a *kofia*, a Zanzibari man's version of a Pillbox hat, emerges from the driver's side. He moves around and opens the back, picking up our backpacks and carefully stowing them.

"We will take you to your hotel in Stone Town," she says, "and then in a few days when we are finished with the training, you are welcome to stay with me at Palm Beach."

She owns a gorgeous little bed and breakfast overlooking the Indian Ocean on the other side of the island in the village of Bwejuu. A reef separates the turquoise waters from the mysterious dark blue. When the tide is out, you can swim in the tide pools and see all kinds of colorful fish and red and orange starfish. The beach is home to cows that munch on piles of scattered seaweed. The regal Maasai warriors sporting scarlet blankets travel the beach on their way to guard the other hotels and restaurants.

We arrive at the Zanzibar Serena Hotel – a restored, historic whitewashed stone building. Mama Naila hugs us goodbye, and we walk up the broad steps into the hotel's lobby. Inside, the ceiling's dark beams contrast with the whitewashed walls, making it feel more like a majestic hall than a lobby. A tall man in a gold and orange vest and a shining smile greets us, "Hujambo," he says as he reaches for our bags. He guides us over to the front desk and waits patiently behind us as we check in. Then up two flights of stairs and down an open-air hallway. I can see the ocean inside the arched whitewashed frame at the end of the hall. The water is a pool of blue sapphires. A couple of *dhows* transverse, drifting beyond view. He inserts the key into the cast-iron lock of the ebony wood door and gently pushes it aside so we can walk through. Our room is sweet and small. I notice the curtain twisting in the breeze and walk over to the balcony door, opening it. I look down to see a large key-shaped swimming pool. Off to the left, the ocean sparkles as the dhow's lateen sails glide by.

I love Zanzibar! *I'm home.*

The porter leaves our bags on the cushioned bench and exits into the hallway.

"What a pretty room!"

"Yes, but it has only one bed. How are we going to work this?" Doug complains.

Caught up in the moment and the novelty and beauty of the hotel, "Let's not worry about that now," I say, "We can figure that out later. Do you want to go for a swim or get something to eat?"

"Let's go get something to eat."

We peek inside the five-table restaurant across the street, but it looks more formal, like a dinner place. So, we keep walking. Not far from the hotel, as everything is fairly close in Stone Town, we find a restaurant with outside seating that serves pizza, fresh juices, and beer.

Quiet at first, we sidestep one another, talking about the scenery, the humidity and how great it is to see Mama Naila again. Finally, the conversation moves toward what happened in the Seychelles.

With as much condemnation as he can muster, "So, did you sleep with him again?"

"Actually, no. We just hung out. He took me to different parts of the island. I got to see how the locals live, I guess."

Except for the disappointing love affair part and the terrible sex, I enjoyed my time with Sunley. I got to see the island through his eyes instead of the eyes of a tourist. He introduced me to a new world, a world of porn and poverty and heroin.

I asked Sunley why he had a padlock on his room since he only lived with his mother. He said the police broke in and stole all his porn videos so now he keeps it locked. He said porn is a big thing on the island and those videos are a valuable commodity. I didn't understand why. The drugs turn him off and don't allow him to feel anything, especially himself. Porn is probably a secret, safe way to feel his sexuality and his power, without having to actually be intimate. Poverty does weird things to people. I noticed that Sunley called me his "girl" and paid for everything, even though he was poor. Yet he has a great hate for authority and resents those with money.

"So, what did you do on La Digue?" I ask.

"I met an Italian woman on the boat who was going to the island," he pauses with a smile. "She was photographing the island." He continues, "And, she has HIV."

This made me silently freak out about Sunley.

"Really? Did you sleep with her?"

"No, she has a boyfriend," he says with disappointment.

I wonder.

Part of me is glad nothing happened, the part of me that hasn't let go.

"I met some Russian porn stars with old men at their side. I guess they do a lot of filming on the Seychelles," he comments.

"Wow, I heard some Russians have a lot of money, and there are so many beautiful women in Russia. So, what did you do then?"

"It was very boring." Sadness clouding his face, "It is an island for couples. There were a lot of honeymooners doing 'couple' things. I felt lonely and angry."

He continues, "I'm glad I had time away from you. I was so angry. I wanted to kill you. I've cooled down a bit."

"I'm sorry I hurt you, Doug." I look deep into his eyes. He reaches out across the table and takes my hands in his. Warmth spreads up my arms.

Except for the weight in my chest, it almost feels like old times.

But I know it isn't.

I can't let go of the guilt. I now feel I must be even more of a pleaser. That I don't deserve to feel happy because of what I have done. Even though I am at my most favorite place on earth.

Somehow, I deserve to be punished for the horrible person I have become.

Cows on the beach near Palm Beach Inn, Bwejuu, Zanzibar.

Dhows-a view from the Zanzibar Hotel Serena.

chapter nineteen

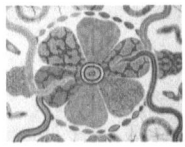

A tarot-card reader once told me that my life was like those women on the television show, Stepford Wives.

Except, the majority of women on my street had grey hair. I didn't have a clue what she was talking about. I'd never watched the show. She summed it up for me, perfect and boring.

Inside of all this beauty and space, I'm trapped inside a life that is not my own making.

When did I become boring?

As a little girl, I loved horses. I had a horse, Miss, and she had a particularly stubborn and independent spirit. We would battle about putting the saddle on her back. And fight to have the bit of the bridle in her mouth. My dad invested in a hackamore bridle that I could easily slip over her soft, alfalfa-scented nose. Then, I would climb onto her back. We'd thunder across the field feeling the wind in our faces.

We were free.

The tarot-card reader also told me the time would come when Doug and I would part ways. Back then, I couldn't feel that to be true. I didn't think he would ever cease to part of my life. But early in the marriage, I started noticing how disconnected from each other we had become. How I didn't like the reality of who he was. *At what point did my idea of him change? And at what point had I failed to live up to the idea he had of me?*

In fact, I thought, I'd call it quits about a year into our marriage. I thought time would heal the grief Doug felt after his mom's death. *He needs more time, that's all.* But as the years went by, I became more and more resentful.

He seemed like a mannequin inside a human carcass and probably wouldn't respond even if I pinched him. Buried in his world most of the time, he didn't hear me when I spoke. Sometimes, I would ask him, "What did I just say?" And he would repeat it back like a Mynah bird.

When we lived together, he toiled daily on his computer. I think mostly so he didn't have to interact with me. He didn't appear to care what I did with my time, as long as I didn't interrupt him, and as long as I was available when he wanted a playmate.

I continue to persuade myself of my charmed life and work myself into an exhausted stupor. I have everything I want. Of course, my marriage, could be better, but who doesn't have issues in their relationships? I have the freedom to come and go as I please. Surely that's more important than experiencing the drama of some tumultuous erotic love life. Passion would be nice. But I'm not a spring chicken anymore.

I repeat this mantra day in and day out until an eternity of mediocrity invisibly passes me by.

I'm almost too asleep to remember what our life was like a long time ago, before we were married.

And, before his mother got sick.

chapter twenty

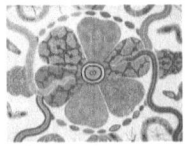

We lived in a converted garage below the central part of his mother's outstretched house near downtown Santa Fe, New Mexico.

Unemployed, Doug searched for a job that would apply his college education. Meanwhile, through his connections, he found me a couple of restaurant jobs. I didn't have a green card, so I worked under the table. And due to my blonde hair and blue-eyed camouflage, we hoped I wouldn't be discovered as an "illegal."

As the months passed, I began to feel like an intruder in the mother-son relationship.

I wasn't invited along to certain family events.

His mom initiated private discussions with Doug. They would leave me standing alone while they went into another room to talk. She was a good military strategist and kept me close, watching us with her hawk eyes to see where she could force in a wedge.

Years later, I learned she had planned to buy me off, until Doug's dad intervened.

Her plan backfired.

I had come between her and Doug.

The stress from being smiled at while being resented caused severe gallstone attacks. My once white skin turned the color of a ripe pear, and I couldn't eat anything without painful late-night spasms.

I constantly feared discovery by the authorities on a kitchen raid, though they were usually looking for the swarthier illegal immigrants.

I decided to go back home to Canada.

After I took measures to restore my health, I returned to school, studying Spanish and Latin American Studies. I planned to study a year in Canada and from there, apply to some schools in the USA and gain legal entry into the country.

I was accepted at two schools, one in Austin and the other in Albuquerque.

I wanted to go to Austin, but Doug landed a teaching job in Albuquerque and wanted to remain near his beloved Santa Fe.

Somehow, Doug and I survived the long distance, visiting back and forth every couple of months.

Settled in Albuquerque, the one-hour drive distanced us from maternal interference, and our relationship flourished. School and work kept us busy, but we managed to have weekends to explore New Mexico and the neighboring states.

My life was good, and the confusing feelings about my place of belonging in the family crept away. Doug's mother even took me to Mexico for a week with her girlfriends. I began to truly feel like a daughter to her.

That June, Doug and I got engaged.

Excitedly, I proudly showed off my sparkling sapphire ring. And we announced that we would get married the following summer solstice.

Doug enjoyed teaching Spanish, but it didn't pay very much. I had a scholarship, so my financial contribution was minimal. When his school offered a place to live on campus, we jumped at the opportunity.

There was only one catch.

It was a Presbyterian religious school. And we had to be married for us to live there.

On August 19th, 1999, on a hot and dry day a week before school started, we drove to the courthouse in sleepy downtown Albuquerque, wearing shorts, t-shirts, and flip-flops. In a cramped, dimly-lit office with a tall American flag looming in the corner, we were married unceremoniously fifteen minutes later.

We skipped out of the office, driving to Garcia's on 4th Street where we celebrated with burritos smothered in green chile. Excited by our newest adventure, we climbed into the old army-green Toyota pickup truck with no air conditioning and drove to Moab, Utah.

We were enjoying a short honeymoon in our playground of Moab's hot, red sandstone until Doug called his mother to tell her the news.

As he was on the phone, I leaned patiently against the wall, watching Doug twist the metal phone cord around his fingers.

"But Mom, we're on our honeymoon, and we've only been here a couple of days, and we don't have to be back for another two."

He listened in silence.

"Well, what did they say?"

Waiting.

"I know your back has been hurting, but there is nothing I can do. Have you been for a massage?" Doug suggested.

She had been in back pain for a couple of months and thought she needed a new mattress. When that didn't help, she went to her doctor. After a series of tests, her doctor couldn't find anything wrong with her and continued with more tests. She had gone for another test that day, and the results wouldn't be back until early the following week.

"Okay, I'll tell her if that's what you want. Bye, Mom. I love you," he said and put the receiver back in the pay phone's cradle.

The furrow between his eyebrows spoke concern, but the irritation in his voice said something else.

"Mom wants us to come home and see her. Her back is hurting a lot."

"Now?"

His shoulder angled toward me, "Yes." His eyes looked off across the valley.

"But we just got here!" I didn't want to go back. I was having too much fun exploring and discovering dinosaur footprints in the sandstone. I felt angry that he always did what she asked of him.

But I kept it to myself.

"Okay." I lied. "We better pack up our tent, then."

The nine-hour drive back to Santa Fe with truck windows rolled all the way down, the hot air encircled me. I felt as if I were inside a dryer, spinning. Until I fell asleep to a reggae song on an overplayed, stretched-out tape.

We spent the next couple of days in Santa Fe with his mother until we needed to return to Albuquerque to work and school.

A couple of days later we received the news.

Doug's mom had stage IV cancer that had metastasized to her bones.

I was in disbelief. *How could the doctor miss that?*

We drove up to Santa Fe to be with her, joining her for an appointment with the oncologist. She asked him how much time she had left. The oncologist told her in a flat voice, "Six months."

I was furious she even wanted to know.

She had given up before she even tried.

With his mother's death sentence, Doug immediately went to work to search for alternative cures besides the chemo and radiation that she reluctantly agreed to do.

For about a month, Doug and I commuted back and forth while trying to juggle school and work. She asked Doug to move back so he could be with her. It was my last semester at university, and I stayed in Albuquerque, driving her old gold Volvo to see them on the weekends.

Doug's quest for a cure became his obsession. He immersed himself in research and the world of doctors' appointments.

I was pushed to the outskirts of this new world he created.

He withdrew his love from me, closing me out like wooden shutters during hurricane season. Never to open his heart again.

I kept hoping that time would heal him and he would open up to me again.

I should be more understanding.

I felt betrayed and abandoned. My insides roiled in hot magma soup.

I was bitterly glad when she died, almost to the day the oncologist had predicted. Now, maybe I would get my husband back. But she won. Like the ghostly arroyos of the Southwest, Doug's once lively eyes remained dry of tears for the next seven years.

chapter twenty-one

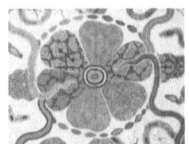

One day, I decided to sort through my closet and delete some things from my life I no longer needed or used.

The first box I opened – big mistake – was filled with journals. I wrote in journals only when I traveled. I wanted to record all my adventures. It never crossed my mind to record what my daily life was like. In my mind, nothing of consequence happened. Certainly, not exciting enough to waste ink on. That changed much later when I needed to explore my feelings with no one but me to judge.

I picked up a navy, soft-cover notebook covered with cherry blossoms. I flipped through it quickly. A couple of ticket stubs from Japanese temples fell onto the floor. I replaced them amongst the wide-lined pages and set it back in the box.

I next selected a thicker hardbound journal. I opened it up somewhere near the middle where I'm complaining about all the things I don't like about Doug. I look to the inside jacket and look for the date. 2000.

Are you serious!

I delve into the box and pick up another journal. I whiz through, glancing at what I wrote. The year, 2006.

No!

I can't believe it. I'm still complaining about those very same things. Nothing has changed. I keep talking about it, talking about all the problems in our relationship. I never dare to change it. I've been complaining about the same things for years, like a stuck record. I have proof. Right here, in writing.

After the disbelief passes, I'm disgusted with myself. I feel pathetic, and I want to bury myself in the box with my journals.

chapter twenty-two

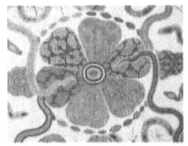

I don't recall how it all came about, but sometimes a good friend can see you in a way you don't want to see yourself.

That's how Sandy is; she read through me like I had invisible skin, right inside of my sleeping heart.

Sandy, a wildfire of a woman with blazing periwinkle eyes, appeared at the office one day. It's interesting how commiserating with someone can make you fast friends. The massage clients are consistent and the doctor pleasant enough, but we bitched about how the place operates and how we have to downplay ourselves and our skills to keep our diva of a boss happy. Between clients, we laughed and shared our angst.

Sandy and I became sisters.

She's a single mom, raising three teenage daughters on her own. Their father committed suicide. She divorced her second husband who left her broke and jaded. Her mom pays her mortgage, and for the girls' education, so she is lucky. Naturally, she's down on men. But mostly, she's tired with the way her life has turned out.

I can totally relate. I imagine myself high above, floating in a hot-air balloon. *How did I end up here? How can this be my life?*

On our days off, Sandy and I hike the ponderosa-covered Sangre de Cristo mountains nestled behind her house. Walking and talking, and dreaming of a more exciting life than the one we currently live.

Her house is conveniently close to work. I often spend time there, eating her eclectic renditions of quesadillas and omelets. When she wants a little bit of countryside, she visits me in her bing-cherry red car with black tinted windows and a failing battery to join me to walk my dogs out amongst the cholla cacti and juniper bushes. Often, we sit silently atop the old train trestle that divides the brittle grassed savannah into two mounds, watching for antelope as the sunset dazzles the dusky sky and gently vanishes for the night.

The walk back becomes an inaudible padding of feet on the dusty cow path, plodding along lost in the thoughts that bounce around inside our heads.

My thoughts halt for a moment when Sandy blurts, "Georgina, I think you should go to Peru with me."

Intrigued, yet with a noncommittal, "Maybe," I answer. "But I was thinking of going back to the Seychelles." A moment of silence and I continue, "To tell you the truth, I don't know what the hell I want to do," pausing, "I'll think about it."

For a few more yards up the path, I get lost in the fantasy of me and Sunley and how things could work out. Sandy's voice draws me back to the desert.

"In November," she says. "I'll be going to Peru in November. Come with me."

"For how long?" It's not like I think Doug and I will be any closer to working out our relationship by then. I'm not so hopeful about it.

"Probably a week or so. I can't afford to take too much time off work with all the credit-card debt and Christmas around the corner."

My mind wanders off to thoughts of a cold beer and a dinner of dark chocolate ice-cream, and I smile at her, "I'll think about it and let you know."

Walking up the crunching gravel driveway, slimy tracks of dog drool drip down the back of my knees. Jonas, my Great Dane, insists on tucking his nose for safety in the crook of my leg. We enter the shadowed kitchen as the last of the day's light lingers a moment longer. I open the fridge and pull out two chilled Negra Modelos, passing one to Sandy.

With an embarrassed laugh, "Isn't this the healthiest dinner you've ever had?"

"It does contain almost all the B vitamins you'd ever need. Plus, I'm trying to lose weight." She looks down at her jeans and grabs the outside seam. "My thighs are so flabby."

I raise my right eyebrow at her. Sandy is as lean as a willow bush in winter. She doesn't even have to wear a bra. Unlike myself, with a full-bloom figure. I wouldn't dream of not wearing a bra. We head outside and plop ourselves down in the cold cast iron chairs. I push off a shoe, allowing my tired feet to breathe and toss my legs up onto the metal table and let out a big sigh. The beer starts its relaxing effects on my body and my tongue.

I natter on about Sunley and how he wants to come to the States. But mostly, about how I really want to get out of here.

"If you come to Peru, you might see things differently. You never know what you might want to do after that!"

She's right.

Since I don't know what I want, I'm open to other possibilities. My habit is to do something, anything, to stop the feeling of quiet desperation gnawing away at my insides.

As if reading my mind, she says in her older-sister voice, "Well you should do something. It doesn't look like your relationship with Doug is going anywhere. It is draining you of your life force, and you are becoming lackluster. You could find someone who is more supportive and loving."

I defend myself, "Yeah, but I'm scared. What if it doesn't get any better than this? What if all relationships are like this? Then, I will just be doing the same thing with someone else and maybe not realize it until I am old and ugly and then who will want me?"

"Don't be ridiculous! You are beautiful and interesting and who wouldn't want to be with you? You won't know until you make a change, anyway. If you and Doug are meant to be, you will be."

"I'm quite sure we're not meant to be. Especially since we separated, again. I'm scared,"

One thing I appreciate about Sandy is her insight into life that her additional years have piled upon her. But she has a palpable heaviness about her, and her past ghosts shadow her wherever she goes. Seasoned by time and hardship, she resents anyone whose life appears to carry a sense of ease and joy. She judges and criticizes harshly those who haven't punished themselves into a casket of martyrdom and considers them lacking in depth. Never mind men! She rarely utters a kind word about any man and most she deems weak and worthless. I often wonder what she honestly thinks about me. But I never ask for fear she will decimate my already fragile self-esteem.

It's late, and of course, Sandy's car doesn't start. I hook up the cable and give her a jump and a prayer that she will arrive safely home. Delaying going back inside the lonely house, I watch Sandy speed down the driveway, leaving behind her a choking dust cloud. Goosebumps creep up my bare legs, and I decide to go inside to put on my red fleece jacket, so I can sit outside a while longer and enjoy one more beer before bed.

The effects of the beer leave my mind slightly altered and my body tingling numb.

I think about Sandy's invitation to Peru. A couple of months earlier she had returned from her first trip to Peru. She went to a healing center in the Amazon jungle to work with a shaman and drink *ayahuasca*. I didn't know what the heck ayahuasca was, but she said it is a plant medicine and called it, "vine of the soul" or "vine of the dead." None of this meant a thing to me, but she came back with sparkling eyes, looking ten years younger. She sold me on that alone!

I wanted to feel the way she looked, brand new and shiny.

I guess I was looking for an excuse for adventure; something new and exciting.

And, something I hadn't a clue about.

chapter twenty-three

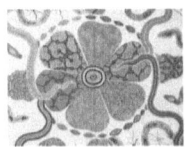

With the hectic summer now over, work has slowed down enough so that my inner chaos chatters on, giving me monkey-mind.

I drift across the idea of going to Peru once again.

I can't decide if I want to go, but I am absolutely bored with myself and my life. You know it's a bad sign when you are so bored with yourself that you fear everyone around you feels the same boredom with you, too.

I work with Sandy a couple of days later. "I've considered going to Peru with you." Wishing I hadn't mentioned it and the doubts rushed in.

She jumps up and down excitedly, "We're going to have this great adventure together. You won't regret this, you'll see." She adds breathlessly, "There isn't much time left. It starts in a couple of weeks, and you have to fill out an application. I can email the center and make sure it isn't too late for you."

Surprised, I exclaim, "Application! It sounds like I am applying to college or something!"

I always tend to leave things to the last second. It is my way of testing fate, to see if I am meant to do something. I figure if it is meant to be it will happen, no matter what. Planning stresses me out, so I do as little as possible.

I leave all the decisions to Sandy since she has experience with Peru and ayahuasca. I don't care one way or another. I usually have a backup plan, anyway. The little voice in my head reminds me, "If it doesn't work out I can always go another time. Or maybe, I am supposed to go to Africa." There I go again in rambling confusion about what to do with my life!

Sandy calls me the next day, "They said it is a little short notice, but they have space for you. I printed off the application, and you need to fax it right away. You also have to wire money to their bank. I haven't done that yet either, so we can do it together if you want."

I drive to her house and pick up the application. I flip through its numerous pages, feeling overwhelmed. They ask more questions than at the doctor's office. Why do they need to know all this stuff? They wanted to know about every physical issue I ever had in my life. Then they want to know if I am crazy, and if so, how crazy? *What am I getting myself into?*

"They use this to weed out people."

Great! Now, I am worried I won't get accepted to a healing center in the jungle. It's like filling out a job application. Pressure. Remembering the mantra, *if it is meant to be it will happen*.

Procrastinating, I decide I would rather have a cup of tea than fill out the form.

We sit down next to the crackling fire of pinyon logs and select a pack of Tarot cards. This is a definite benefit of having a witchy friend. When in doubt, it's our policy to consult the oracle. Sandy has a plethora of divining tools. We each pull three cards from the Shapeshifter deck. All our cards lie face down. We lift a corner and peek, fearing our destinies will be sealed in stone. But we flip them over, one by one.

"I got the Moon, Strength, and the Quest." She proceeds to read what each card means. "The Moon. Psychic abilities, dreams, deception. Something unforeseen is about to happen."

I give an ominous, "Oooh."

She continues, "Messages from spirit may create a change of consciousness. Psychic talents will unfold if you hold to your spiritual path. Your intuition could reveal some dangerous, dark secret or hidden foes. Dreams can lead you to the right decisions. Look at events and people with a cold eye of reality, or you could be deceived."

Sandy comments, "That is interesting. Ayahuasca takes you into you the dream world and makes you see more clearly." She follows with the Strength card:

"Preparedness, vision, divine help, perception. Being watchful of nature's rhythm, a strengthening of perception and intuition is sure to come. With many internal resources at your disposal right now, this is a time of spiritual vision and physical strength against any opposition."

"Well, I am very glad that card is following the Moon card. At least it sounds like you don't have to worry too much, and you'll be protected if there is deception," I said with a sigh of relief, pointing at the last card.

She continues, "The Quest. Seeking, abandonment, apathy."

"I don't like the sound of this one! What is this one in a regular deck?"

She flips to the back of the book, "It's the eight of cups."

"Oh." All I know about that one is that it is often the end of a relationship.

She reads, "The Quest card indicates a restless quest without a goal in reality; stop and look at your inner motives and the illusion under which you live. Balance the spiritual and the physical, for you have allowed an imbalance to occur, believing that the spiritual is all and neglecting physical responsibilities. Your indecisiveness and refusal to make commitments or rational decisions has created problems in your relationships and perhaps in employment as well."

"So, what do you think all of those mean together, Georgina?"

Not knowing what to say, I pick up the three cards and hold them fan-like in my hand. I tell her, "It could have something to do with you searching for something, and you think you will find it in Peru. And because of what we are going to be doing you will definitely be delving into other parts of your mind. Right? But if you get to a place that seems difficult in some way you will be protected."

"I do like to be in the spirit realm a lot more than working and worrying about credit-card debt; that spoke to me. Okay, Georgina, what did you pull?"

"I got Blindness, the Shapeshifter, and Deception. Okay. Blindness, polarity, fear, transformation. Blindness is a card of anxiety, indecision, impotence, and stalemate, just before a spiritual awakening; the time between blindness and sight. You need to conquer personal blindness and the fear that limits your experience, transmuting and expanding your awareness. Don't be blind to your options or close your eyes to a creative part of yourself. The ultimate cost of denying your inner promptings, deeper feelings, and outer vision is living in a self-limited and restricted world. Like a snake shedding its old habits, you may now find yourself embracing a new path in life."

I take a sip of tea and continue, "The Shapeshifter. A pause, prophetic power. This is a time when everything seems to be in suspension with little or no movement in events. Use this opportunity for self-introspection and careful decisions about the effect of present actions on future desires. A period of possible spiritual expansion, be aware of the unexpected messages in dreams, intuition, and from unexpected sources." I look up from reading, "It sounds like Peru is the right choice for me and perhaps it will push me in one direction or another."

I pick up the last card, "I don't like the sound of this one," I say, scrutinizing the snarling charcoal coyote in the black and white drawing. "It sort of sounds like the Moon card. But looks a lot darker." I pick up the card to show it to her. She arches an eyebrow and hands it back. "It says, spying, loss through deception, wrong choices." I stop reading for a second, "Yuck!"

"Read what it says." Sandy urges.

"Beware of using trickery or deceit, for your actions will be exposed, bringing disfavor and penalties down upon you. Poor past choices may come back to haunt you; face your responsibilities and don't deny them. This may indicate one with whom you are involved who is deceiving you for gain." I pause, thinking about what deception was a part of in my life. I have been mostly clean, well, except for Sunley.

I add, "Interesting how both readings sort of talked about Peru. I am glad that eventually, I will shift out of this stalemate. I am tired of being stuck."

We chat around the fire a while longer. It's getting late, and I need to get home to take the dogs for a walk. I collect the application form and stuff the papers into my purse, and hug Sandy on my way out the door.

Later that evening I take out the crumpled papers and start answering the questions. I had to think back to the year I had my gallbladder taken out. I recollected bouts of depression and suicidal tendencies. Hopefully, this won't jeopardize the application. It is supposed to be healing center, after all. I finish all the contact information and look it over one more time to make sure I didn't miss anything. Tomorrow I will fax it off.

I hurry into town and fax the application. Then I rush to the Wells Fargo bank to wire money to the owner of the center before I have to be at work. I'm a little nervous. It seems awfully expensive. *What if it is a waste of money and a terrible experience?*

With the day of departure fast approaching, I take on extra work to make up for the money I would be missing. My body feels tired. How great it will be to not work for nine days. In the meantime, there is a lot to get ready. I load up on bug spray and anti-itch ointment.

I find a pair of snazzy black rubber boots with gray and green spots all over them, perfect for the jungle! All I need is a raincoat, and I'm set. That night I pack my backpack, trying to stuff in everything. Doug looms over my shoulder; he only came to pick up the dog but he can't help but, give me his advice on how best to pack my bag. I ignore his comments as I try to stuff the awkwardly shaped boots into the bottom of my bag. It will be nice to have a break from him for a little while. It seems as time goes by we have less and less in common with each other. He doesn't understand why I need to go on this trip. I guess I don't know either. But it is something I must do.

I don't sleep very well that night. I worry I didn't set my alarm. Or maybe I set it for P.M. instead of A.M. And, did I pack my passport? So, I get up and check, and yes, it's all there. I toss and turn until the alarm goes off at six-thirty. I'm not supposed to have coffee because there are diet restrictions a couple of weeks before a person takes ayahuasca. But diets have never been something I could adhere to. So, I make myself one last delicious cup of coffee. I justify the steaming cup by reminding myself that I followed all the other rules to the diet: no pork, no spicy food, no beer; that was difficult, but I could do it. And, no sex, which wasn't a problem right now anyway.

Savoring the last drop of my coffee I give Sandy a call to make sure she's out of bed. She doesn't pick up her phone, so she might be out doing some last-minute running around. I'm not worried since we have plenty of time to get to the airport. I throw my backpack into my car, arrive at Sandy's, but her car isn't in the driveway. I open the front door and head on in.

A moment later I get a call.

"I had to run up to my mom's to check on her animals. I'll be there in a minute." She pants into the phone.

"Okay." I'm sitting in the living room. I see her backpack lying on the floor looking rather flat. "Are you packed?"

"No, not yet. But it will only take me a second. Everything is ready to be shoved in. I have to go. There is a cop in the next lane over, and I don't want to get a ticket for talking on my cell phone. Bye." Silence. She hangs up.

I wait patiently, annoyed. Sometimes Sandy's disorganization drives me nuts. I could have been at home fretting and checking for the thirtieth time if I packed my passport or not! I hate waiting. As I was becoming super irritated, she bursts through the door, her homemade knitted green scarf flying out behind her.

Unravelling herself, she apologizes breathlessly, "Sorry I made you wait, but neither of the girls would go up to Mom's and help me with the animals. So I had to do it myself. Those girls expect me to do everything for them, but when I need a favor it is like I asked them to cut off their right leg! I swear, I can't wait until they graduate and I have this space all to myself." Ranting, she continues, "And they want to use my car while I'm gone! Can you believe it?"

"What did you tell them?" Chuckling, I already know the answer.

"Well, I had to since I am not here to drive them around, they will have to get to school and to work. I can't ask my mom to drive them everywhere." She takes a breath, "Can you make me a cup of coffee while I throw my stuff in my bag?"

"Sure," I respond. "Do you need help with anything else?" I add walking to the kitchen to pour water into the kettle before placing it on the stove to boil.

"No, not right now. Thanks," she replies, rummaging through her things like she is looking for something specific.

The kettle whistles. I pour the boiling water into the brown unbleached filter resting on the top of Sandy's travel mug. It sure smells good. I always wonder why coffee's smell is so intoxicating. I bet if you couldn't smell it, it wouldn't taste very good either. I should plug my nose when I drink it to try to get off it. Or maybe I should just enjoy it and not feel guilty about drinking it and how my adrenals are suffering from my addiction.

Sandy tries to shove two packages of rice cakes into the top of her bag.

Feeling a little concerned, "Why are you bringing rice cakes? Don't they feed us?"

She laughs, "Yeah, they feed us. But after a ceremony, there is no food. Sometimes in the middle of the night, I get hungry, so I am bringing them to snack on."

Okay, I think. Eating rice cakes plain like that doesn't sound very appetizing to me at all. But she has experience with this sort of thing, not me.

We load her things into the car. She has an extra bag of clothes she planned to give away to people down there. Her bag of knitting needles and wool explode from a shopping bag. I think that it's an odd thing to take to the steamy jungle. But it is winter here. The hatch of my car overflows like we've been to a rummage sale. I can't believe how much stuff she is taking. I worry I didn't bring enough. I brought some clothes to give away, my journal, and several books, including a dilapidated Spanish dictionary from college classes long ago.

During the hour-long drive to the airport, I start to feel excited. I haven't been on a trip in a while and going to the airport feels like I am about to embark on an adventure. I park the car in the long-term parking lot. Sandy wrangles the bag of wool and needles into her carry on, concentrating not to stab herself. The shuttle pulls up, and the driver makes several trips loading all our bags.

"Where you girls off to?"

Sandy replies, "We are going to the Amazon in Peru."

"Aren't you scared of all the bugs and diseases down there?"

"No, not really, we're prepared," I smile.

"You girls sure are brave."

I find it interesting how nearly everyone I told about my trip said the same thing. Bugs don't scare me. I figure I have traveled into the jungles of Africa and slept in some pretty sketchy places in my life.

This won't be too unfamiliar.

chapter twenty-four

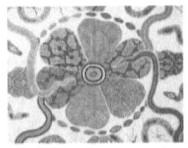

It is six-thirty in the morning.
I clang down the metal stairs onto the tarmac and take in the scenery.

The pinkish-gray sky shimmers as the sun peeks over the jungle canopy. I inhale the fresh, humid air, breathing in the fragrance of the lush green trees. Chilled from the air conditioning on the plane, I pull up the zipper of my jacket.

We enter the airport where the luggage conveyor belt meanders like a wayward stream. I look around to see if our names might be on any of the flaps of cardboard boxes used as welcomes signs. I see nothing that looks like either of our names.

"Sandy, do you know who is coming to pick us up?"

"No, let me look in my bag for the paper I printed out. Just a second. My bag is coming off the plane." A happy rotund man in his fifties approaches us. I hope it is the person meant to meet us.

"Hello, Bonita, how are you?" He flirts, leaning over to kiss Sandy on the cheek.

Her eyes light up in recognition as she answers him in Spanish, "Very well. How are you?" They continue their conversation for a minute longer as he reaches for my bags and hoists them onto a cart. Sandy explains that he was here last time she came to Iquitos. He's a porter. He looks okay, and if Sandy trusts him, I guess he must be all right.

"I want to see if Jon is here from the healing center I went to last time. He is probably here picking up people as well."

I follow her outside.

There is Jon. A bright, blue-eyed gringo with thick leathery skin, about sixty-ish, sporting a tassel of ponytail that hangs down the nape of his neck. He has a rather large collection of silver earrings winding their way up his ears. But my gaze floats across his neck, where several jaguars' worth of impressive fangs encircles it. Sadness floods my heart for the beautiful animals killed to make his trophy.

Jon and Sandy catch up. She tells him we are waiting for someone else to pick us up. At this point, he seems less interested in the conversation. Sandy says good-bye and walks in my direction.

She opens her pack, searching for the paper containing the information about who is picking us up. She extracts a few things, laying them on the warming asphalt. Finally, reaching the bottom of the bag, she says, "I think I forgot the paper at home. But I remember it was out of town a distance. We can ask a taxi driver to take us there."

I agree. How many centers can there be? "Okay, let's get a taxi and ask him to take us on the road where you think it is."

Finding a taxi is not a problem. The drivers can smell your desire for a ride and flock like vultures. We chose a guy who seemed extra helpful. He places our bags carefully in the trunk of his old blue Mazda, and we get in the back seat. We will be well protected. I notice Guadalupe dangling from the rearview mirror in a laminated protective covering. The coiled springs poke through the faded, camel-brown seat cover, and I shift a little closer to Sandy.

A wave of relief passes over me, thinking it won't be long until I can lie down in a proper bed and have a nap. Sandy excitedly chats away in her much better Spanish to the chauffeur as we speed out of the parking lot.

We head out of town, turning right onto the paved road to Nauta. Sandy says, "I think we are going to *Kilometro* 19. The driver knows where that is and it should only take half an hour or so." I lean back wanting to take in the sights, but I am feeling tired and a little cranky. We pass by shacks with palm-frond roofs and rough boards for walls. A few mangy dogs trot down the side of the road. I notice how all the dogs look related to one another. As we drive farther out of town, I see goats eating grass by the side of the road. Women walk like mother ducks with a string of ducklings in tow.

The driver asks us if he can take us to some other places along the way that also do ayahuasca. No! But Sandy says sure. The driver takes a right onto a muddy dirt road. We pass by a few huts, and then he stops. We open the creaky car doors and chickens scatter everywhere. Our driver introduces us to a gringo with sparkling aquamarine eyes and a warm heart who appears to be in his forties. He tells us in a southern drawl through a toothless smile, he is married to a Peruvian and has lived here for about ten years. He says he does ceremonies three times a week if we want to join him, and it only cost twenty-five *Nuevo Soles*.

I look around; judging from the looks of his shack she isn't a very good housekeeper. Or maybe they are just poor. A few chickens fly out as he leads us into a room of sticks with a dirt floor where he does ceremonies. After the brief tour, we let him know we must be on our way. We thank him and get back in the car.

Our driver tells us that we could stop by another place that is not too far up the road. I don't say anything because I know Sandy is game. He pulls off the side of the road and heads up a boggy one-lane path. The mud sticks to everything, and we can't go any farther. He pulls off to the side and informs us it isn't a very long walk. I exit the car and sink into the cool red mud. I look down and roll my pants up, so I don't get completely covered by the stuff. My shoes, Keens, are waterproof so I don't care about them.

A few feet up the road, we meet a young man who works at the place we are headed. The driver informs him of our visit, and the young man runs back from the direction he came. He reappears with a shotgun. He is going to protect the car and our things while we are inside visiting. We take a turn down another muddy path.

On either side are houses with palm roofs and open-sided walls. Apparently, these are the people who work at this center, The Spirit of Anaconda. We pass a woman with a black and brown furry something on her head. I am curious to see what it is. We go over to her and check it out. Her hat is the tiniest little monkey I have ever seen; it sits there with brown eyes looking at us. The woman laughs as we try to pet it and it hides around the crook of her neck. She says, "He's shy."

I ask, "Is it a baby?"

"No, he's full grown," she tells me. Wow, he could fit in the palm of my hand!

Once we get through the entrance of The Spirit of Anaconda, our driver finds someone to show us around. An indigenous man with long hair, who we learn is the shaman there, is hanging out with several gringos. The buildings look well cared for, and he gives us a tour of the interior. He explains what days they hold ceremonies. Sandy tells him we are just curious; thanking him, we slog off through the mud back out to where we parked the car.

The boy with the gun stands up from leaning against the car when he sees us approaching. Once in the car our driver backs out onto the main road and continues toward *Kilometro* 19. A few minutes later, we see a small, white cement marker like a headstone on the side of the road indicating we have reached our destination. He pulls off the road. Thanking him, we pay for our ride and leave him a generous tip, mostly since we aren't quick at currency conversion yet. A couple of small boys race up to the car and lug our bags over to what looks like a *tienda*, a shop.

We inform them we are guests here. They tell us that we need to walk that way, pointing back toward the jungle. It looks far. I see no other buildings in sight, but the boys volunteer to carry our backpacks. I recheck my pants to make sure they are still rolled high enough not to get covered with the sticky clay. Each boy wrestles a pack onto his back, and Sandy and I pick up our carry-on bags.

Mosquitos nibble at my ankles while I'm tramping through the mud. I try to ignore them and pay attention to the scenery instead. We pass by a few swampy areas as we walk over several hills. Finally, I see some buildings ahead. The boys show us into a large room whose walls display many paintings. The artist is the shaman of the center. His art, surreal and otherworldly indicates he is an *ayahuasquero*. A man greets us, and Sandy explains we are guests here for three weeks.

He immediately vanishes.

In his absence, we take a tour.

We explore what appears to be the sleeping area. The rooms look dirty, and the mattresses look old and musty. A shadow skulks away, retreating to a dark corner. It feels strange to me. I can't put my finger on it, but it makes the hair on the back of my neck stand on end.

We return to the main dining area. Awaiting us is the man we met earlier and a blonde woman with a French accent who seems somewhat surprised to see us. She talks to us in Spanish, and it appears she is the one in charge. Sandy gives her the name of the center we think we are at. The blonde woman turns off her friendliness, informing us that this is not the place we are looking for. Part of me is happy since I don't really like the vibe here. But another part of me dreads the thought of our continued search.

A little embarrassed, we get up to leave. Our porters have disappeared, and I am left to carry my own cumbersome backpack in the rain, which helps cool me down.

"I guess the best thing is to go back to Iquitos and find an internet cafe to get the phone number of the people who are supposed to pick us up," I tell her.

"Yeah, we'll have to do that. Let's wait by the road to see if we can hitch a ride into town," says Sandy.

The people at the store look at us like we are a couple of crazy girls with all our bags in the rain. A number of trucks and cars pass by, but no one stops. Eventually, a weighted-down clunker of a car pulls over to pick us up. All the passengers spill out, and Sandy and I get in the back seat. We're sandwiched between two people, plus a child on the lap of the lady to my right. Besides the driver, the front seat has two adults and a couple of kids sitting on laps. With *cumbia* music blasting, the car putts off down the road.

Our ride drops us at the plaza in central Iquitos. We locate an email place and drop our bags inside the door. I decide to check my email, too, and see if I saved information about the center. I did. Sandy also has the same information but needs to go down the street to the *locutorio*, the public pay phone. I decide to watch the bags instead of us both hauling them around.

Sitting outside on the doorstep, I watch the *moto-taxis* screech to the stop lights and then at top speed screech to the next stop light. The air is hot and dusty. My thoughts drift to the jungle where it isn't so dirty, when a long-haired hippy man, wafting of marijuana, approaches me. He is slightly handsome with all his handmade jewelry, white-striped bellbottom pants, and a denim vest.

"*Hola*, what's your name?" he asks, seating himself next to me.

I'm aloof and cool. It is either a pickup line or he is selling something. Possibly, both. "My name is Georgina. And what is yours?"

"My name is Lambda." Turning my hand over he draws with his ragged, uncut nail the Greek symbol on the palm of my hand. "It is a difficult name to remember."

I don't think so especially since he engraved it into my skin.

"I won't forget," I assure him.

"What are you doing here?"

"I am waiting for my friend. She went to make a phone call. She'll be back soon."

"I mean, what are you doing *here*, in Iquitos."

"We are going to a center in the jungle to study plant medicine."

"When will you be back?"

"Next week."

Now we get to the what he is selling. "Would you like to see the jewelry I make?"

Sandy still isn't back, and he seems fairly harmless, so I agree.

He opens his knapsack and displays on the steps the pieces he has made. Beautiful stones interlaced with hemp string and beads. He ties one around my wrist. I tell him it is beautiful, as Sandy approaches us.

She informs me our ride will be here in half an hour and picks up one of Lambda's necklaces.

"I make jewelry, too." She points to the necklaces she wears around her neck.

He gives her a big smile and introduces himself. He then reaches deeper into his pack and pulls out a drawstring pouch. He delves into his pouch, extracting a stone not yet made into jewelry.

"Do you know what kind of stone this is?" he asks Sandy.

It is a royal blue stone, and she answers confidently, "Lapis Azul."

"*Correcto!!*" He responds while he is reaching in for more stones. So their game begins. With each stone he pulls out, he thinks he has stumped her. But Sandy gets each one correct. I am amazed at her knowledge of stones and laugh as he tries to find more and more obscure ones for her to identify.

Just then a moto-taxi drives up to the curb, and a well-fed, sweaty man exits the open side that serves as the door. He asks us our names to confirm we are who he is meant to pick up. He has come for us, but first, he must do an errand.

So, we wait on the steps with Lambda. He asks, "What plants are you studying at the center?"

Sandy replies, "Ayahuasca. Have you tried it?"

With a look of horror, he says, "No, I am afraid to try it."

I'm wondering why when Sandy asks him, "Why are you afraid?"

"I don't want to see *demonios*."

Demonios? Demons? What is he talking about?

"But it is very healing. You should try it sometime," she presses him.

The person who came to pick us up approaches. He gives Lambda a look that says, *you better get out of here. These are my girls*, and reaches down to pick up a bag. He wedges onto the carrying space behind the carriage part of the taxi. Lambda says *adios*, kissing both of us on the cheek and wishes us luck.

chapter twenty-five

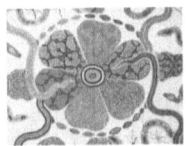

The driver bungee-cords our bags to the metal rack at the back of the moto-taxi.

Once seated inside, he instructs us to hang on to them. I twist to reach behind, gripping the handle of my backpack as the taxi takes off, zooming up to the stop light.

Shouting over the noise of the engine, the driver introduces himself.

"I am Humberto's uncle, Julio."

Leaving the dust and noise of the city behind, we head out of town into the jungle. The road narrows the farther we go; starting on a two-lane road, to a gravel road, and eventually, the moto-taxi squeezes onto a golden, sandy walking path. We pass by small villages as shoeless children run out to stare at the two white women bouncing by. We wave, and they run alongside the taxi waving back at us like we are the most exciting thing they have ever seen.

Finally, we make a turn into a canopy-covered trail that leads to the healing center. On a bench under an open hut, a group of people sit, awaiting our arrival. They rise to greet us and take our bags. We follow behind them as they lead us to our little house nestled between the huge trees.

We climb the steps to our casita and leave our muddy shoes inside the door. The hut is spacious. The wooden walls come up to about chest height, and the rest is covered with green mosquito screening that joins the poles at the bottom of the palm roof. Air circulates through the open roof, leaving the room cool.

The casita contains two beds. Each is covered with a black and white handmade textile. Stripped-bare tree branches and green fishing string hold up a white muslin mosquito net. The bathroom, an attached room to the back, is sort of an afterthought. However, there is a real porcelain toilet and a real shower head. Humberto shows us how to use the toilet by scooping water out of the large bucket next to the toilet and pouring it into the basin. Toilet paper goes into a trash can. Simple enough. Humberto says goodbye and leaves us to unpack and rest awhile before our lunch.

"This is pretty nice," I say out loud.

"It is nicer than the room I had over at Jon's place. There, I had to walk outside to an outhouse to use the bathroom. Which bed do you want?"

"You can choose first. It doesn't matter to me. If the mattress is horrible, I've got my Thermarest."

"I will take this one, then," she says putting her bags near one end of the double bed.

I move over to the far wall and throw my travel pillow on the smaller bed. I plunk down with a bounce. I'm glad I brought my own pillow. The pillow provided for me is as hard as a block of wood. The foam mattress feels comfortable, and I close my eyes for what seems like a nanosecond.

A knock comes at the door and startles me awake from my nap. Both Sandy and I get up to see who is there. A dark-haired beauty dressed in a pink and turquoise satin blouse smiles at us from the doorway. From behind her black skirt, embroidered with lines similar to the bed covering, peeks a large brown-eyed girl.

"Hi. My name is Maria," she announces cheerfully. "And this is my daughter, Lupe. We came to tell you your lunch will be ready in twenty minutes. The dining room is across the bridge where you came in."

"Okay. Thanks, Maria," we chime. Maria and Lupe descend the steps and wave good-bye.

"I'm going to take a quick shower and put shorts on. It's really hot, and I'm feeling sticky from all that traveling," I inform Sandy.

"I will take one after you, then." She sits down on the bed and pulls out clothes from her pack.

The cold-shower water refreshes me, and I start to feel more awake. I slap the odd mosquito that has the nerve to land on me. I make a quick mental note to shower in the middle of the day when they aren't out in full force.

On the way to the dining hall, we pass by three other similar-looking huts, all painted with the black-lined design. I learn later this black-lined style is the art of the Shipibo Indians, which is the tribe Humberto and his family belong to.

We cross a small, red stream the color of South African Rooibos tea, snaking its way through the property. Climbing the steps that lead into the dining hall, we enter through a crookedly-hung screened wooden door. Shipibo textiles function as tablecloths, covering long wooden tables placed in the center of the room. The back walls, draped with more textiles, brighten the simplicity of the space.

I choose a handmade wooden chair facing the outside. Sandy sits next to me. The cook arrives with plastic containers of chicken cooked with onions and tomatoes, rice, and mixed vegetable. This looks so good! We have a pitcher of fresh pineapple juice to drink. That's what I love about being in the tropics. Fresh fruit that tastes like fruit. Not the tasteless, hard, cardboard fruit of the United States.

After the tasty meal, I want to go back and continue my nap. But they have an orientation planned for us. Humberto begins with an official introduction; his sister Maria and Lupe, who now wiggles shyly next to her mom, and to the cook, Juanita. He continues, presenting the rest of his family; Julio who came to pick us up, his mom Inez, his dad don Juan and his cousin Emilio. With the who's who formalities now complete, Juanita slips back into the kitchen.

He informs us that at four o'clock a shaman will come to our casita to talk with us about what we want to get out of the ceremonies. As he continues his filibuster, all I can think of is that I really need to go to sleep! Eventually, he ends his monologue, and I leave. Sandy decides to stay and talk with them a while longer.

Lying on my bed, I think, *Why AM I here?* I still don't know. Health-wise, I am pretty good, although I do suffer terribly from menstrual cramps. Maybe I'll focus my intention on that.

Sandy told me that it is very important to go into the ceremony with an intention so that you have something to focus on. Her roommate from Jon's retreat center made that an important pre-ceremony activity and Sandy was passing that on to me.

I get out my journal and start writing my intentions onto the pages.

Okay. *What do I want to get out of this ceremony?* I write, "To heal my body of menstrual cramps and to know what to do in my life."

That was simple enough.

I close my eyes and make the intention into a mantra. Within a few minutes, I drift off to sleep.

I awake to the flicker of candlelight. Sandy carefully rotates the dried sage leaves through the orange flame. Blowing it out, she floats through the room, leaving trails of smoke in all the corners.

Having purified the room's energy, she approaches me, "Stand up. I am going to sage you, too."

I get up, holding my arms out in a cross formation. She wafts the smoke around my face and head, under my arms and over the rest of my body. With my energy field cleansed, she hands me the burning bundle of sage, "My turn."

Carefully catching falling embers, I do the same for her. Finished, I pass the dried sage back to her. She blows smoke under her bed before she returns it to the glass jar on the altar.

"I always feel nervous before a ceremony," she confesses.

"Why? You've done this a bunch of times and know what to expect."

"I know. I just do. I can't really explain why. Maybe it is because it is such an intense experience. Just thinking about drinking the ayahuasca makes me shiver," she says, making a face and shimmying her body like she had a mouthful of something horrible.

I laugh at her.

"You just wait and see. You won't be laughing tomorrow!"

chapter twenty-six

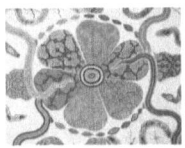

About an hour and a half later, I understand Sandy's anxiety when the ayahuasca pummels me like a freight train.

I swear, I'm going to die.

I'm freezing cold even with the blanket swaddling me. I am vomiting truckloads, yet I haven't eaten in nine hours. My teeth rattle in my skull as my entire body trembles uncontrollably.

This goes on for eternity.

I have lost all relationship to time. Eventually, the physical sensations lessen. I realize I won't die. But I imagine at the very least I will be a candidate for *One Flew Over the Cuckoo's Nest*.

Back safe in our hut, I'm flopped on my bed like cooked spaghetti noodles. I inform Sandy, "I'm never, EVER doing ayahuasca again."

She laughs at me. "Of course you will!"

Hell no!

She's right.

With a day between ceremonies, I decompress. I begin feeling lighter and slightly brighter. Almost as if that horrible experience has become a water-colored memory. Like women who have given birth, they completely forget about the painful contractions.

I suppose I can manage another ceremony.

But, I wasn't expecting the same violent agony to continue the second time around. Finally, during the fourth ceremony, relief is in store, and I am rewarded with an uplifting spiritual experience.

The *maloca's* planked walls melt into the staccato sounds of insects at night. In my vision, I am transported to a moist patch of soft decaying leaves on the jungle floor. The vibration of the insect's voices, the messages from the massive trees, and the nurturing warmth of Mother Earth herself flood my DNA.

I lie listening, intrigued by their song. Hundreds of voices from creatures and nature spirits sing out. I feel cradled in a net of love extending to and from me on filaments of light. In my vision, I look out across the world. I perceive myself as a light strung next to an infinite number of lights, all enclosed in unique bodies; all powered by Source, the Creator, God, the Universe.

I can't remember feeling this sense of completeness for as far back as I can remember.

I just had a revelation! This feeling encapsulating me and surging through my cells is LOVE! With the One Mind, with All, with our Source. I never knew there was such intense and unconditional love. Up until this experience, I believed in the illusion that I was inconsequential; I was a speck of insignificance in the gigantic multi-universe. At this moment I experience deep in my bone marrow, my connection, my unity, with All.

I know the truth about myself. My luminescence lights up the vast sky with brilliance.

I am beginning to remember who I am.

Mud bath on first Peru trip.

Hugging an anaconda at the wildlife sanctuary.

chapter twenty-seven

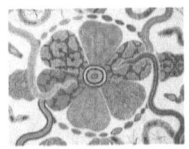

At home, the brilliance and changes that had bloomed within me seemed to wither away within a few days.

Somehow, I regress.

I have terror within me. Like ants must feel when the earth begins to shake and shiver right before an earthquake. I don't know how to quell this doom I feel rising.

I seek out comfort with the familiar. I jump back into work. And I jump right back in bed with Doug, even though my gut tells me this is absolutely the wrong thing to do. I let my fears and my mind convince me this is what I need.

But, by the end of the first week home, I become increasingly miserable. As if I'm sluicing down the drain or some kind of hole I cannot escape unless I do something.

I feel an ache inside. A disconnect from what seemed so permanent and real when I was in the jungle.

I am starving for more. My brief four-ceremony encounter with ayahuasca isn't enough.

Within a week of returning home, I book another, longer, trip to Iquitos.

I let Sandy know about my plan. Of course, she wants to come along. We make our reservations at the healing center for three weeks this time, and we will be leaving in a month.

After our travel plans are set in stone, Sandy begins to act weird.

She starts ignoring me and making up excuses why she can't hang out with me like we have. My feelings hurt, I don't understand why she is so distant and icy. We pretend everything is the same. But it isn't. Something between us has changed.

But, I'm not in on the secret.

A week before we are due to leave, I'm at her house sipping tea next to the blazing fireplace. Our feet are up on the brick mantel, our legs forming a v-shape and our big toes nearly touching.

Suddenly like an Arctic storm blowing in out of nowhere, she rants. "I'm not your mother. I hated it when we were in Peru, and you leaned on me. You expected me to help you with everything."

Aghast, I pull my feet off the brick and plant them on the floor, bracing myself for tempest unleashed.

"I'm not your mother! It's time for you to grow up! When we go back, I'm going to get my own casita. You will have to sleep on your own."

Reeling from the frigid tornado that has swept the room, I sit there in silence. *What was that all about?* I certainly didn't want her mothering me. I didn't see her in that way at all. I admit, I did follow in her footsteps, only because she seemed to know what the hell she was doing when it came to ayahuasca. And I hadn't a clue. I didn't realize that was a burden to her.

"Okay. That's fine." I do my best to conceal the hurt. "I'll get my own casita."

The week goes by like I'm struggling through quicksand.

I avoid her. At work, I walk on eggshells in Sandy's presence. And, I am tooth-achingly sweet and cheerful. I still don't know what I did to stir up such anger in her. This is going to be awkward, traveling together. Pretending to be friends when I'm waiting for the next time she'd lash out at me.

It is as if I have insight into another side of Sandy. A side I don't really like.

That night, I have the weirdest dream. I dream I am a lioness in the dark woods. By my feet lies a lion cub that I protect. On the edge of the woods, a black jaguar appears. I become wary and protective as the big cat encircles us. A road with grass sprouting up the middle divides us from a scene of an assortment of African animals. They walk single file, one behind the other, away from me. Then the scene switches to a barn full of human slaves and part-human part-animal creatures. I am disgusted as I watch the bestiality occurring right in front of my eyes. Strange sexual scenes straight out of Hades itself. Then these slaves and creatures are loaded onto stock trailers while the slave driver whips them from behind.

I wake up feeling very disturbed. I don't understand what all the grotesque scenes mean.

But I know I must protect myself from very something dark.

chapter twenty-eight

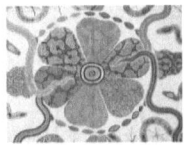

Back on familiar ground at the healing center, I march to the very last cabin, nestled right under the large, lush jungle canopy; cabin number five.

I smile to myself, I will be hugged by the trees at night.

I block Sandy from my mind.

Part of me likes the idea of being alone. But part of me will miss talking with her at night when I can't sleep. She is in casita number two, up the path and not too far from the kitchen.

I focus on unpacking my things.

I toss my backpack on the bench against the far wall. I take out my toothbrush and brush two days' worth of fuzz off my teeth. Next, I take out the handmade soap my stepmom made me. I place it along with my shampoo on the one-by-four board that serves as a shelf.

An hour later, I hear a timid tapping on the wooden frame of my screen door. I look over my shoulder from where I sit on the bed.

"Can I come in?" Sandy asks. Standing on the steps, she waits politely until I answer.

"Yes," I reluctantly agree. She pushes the door open and closes it carefully so it won't slam. And maybe, to buy more time.

"I'm so sorry. I've been such a bitch to you," she sniffles. Mascara has left dirty tracks down her cheeks. "Can I sleep in here with you?"

I put my hands on my hips and gruffly say, "What happened to your casita? What happened to wanting to sleep by yourself and not mothering me?"

"Well, I don't want to sleep there by myself anymore." She pauses.

"Why not?" I can tell she's hiding something. "Isn't this how you wanted it?"

I can see the struggle ensue between her eyes and her mouth. I don't care. She wants to have it her way, she better come up with a good reason.

She takes a deep breath. "Well, I just had sex with Humberto," she blurts.

My eyes practically pop out of their sockets.

"In there, on the floor." She points over to casita number two. "It was terrible." More tears poured down her face. "And then... he left. I feel so used." She mumbles, "I'm sorry."

Judging her harshly, I think *What is she doing?*

This is the second time she has had sex with him.

The first time was when we were overnight in Iquitos, waiting for our flight out the next day. She left. She said it would only be for a couple of hours. But she didn't come back until early the following morning.

I was so worried about her. And very annoyed. She left me in charge of a baby monkey that she had bought at the animal sanctuary. It was a tiny little monkey. The baby version of the one we saw hiding in the woman's neck when we first arrived in Iquitos months ago. It really needed to be taken care of by its mama, which I became for the night. I fed it bananas and held it and cleaned up after it. I didn't sleep much; you know how babies are.

"I don't know what I was thinking," she said then, taking the little creature in her hands and bringing it close to her face to kiss. "I'd better take him back. There is no way they will let me leave the country with a monkey."

With anger-tinted curiosity, I asked, "How was your night?"

"Okay. I rented a room, and we had sex. Nothing great."

I thought it weird that she paid for the room.

So here she is again, having sex with Humberto. We aren't even supposed to have sex on our *dieta*. I sit on my bed, pissed. For the first time, I realize perhaps she needs me more than I need her. I pause a minute longer, feeling all the conflicting waves crashing into each other.

But my heart opens to her. "I suppose."

"Thank you!" she says excitedly and gives me a hug.

She turns around and goes outside, letting the door slam. A few minutes later, she returns with her backpack, lugging it up each creaking wooden plank.

As she unpacks, I lie down for a short nap.

chapter twenty-nine

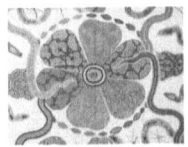

Rudely awakened by a squawking ruckus, I get up to see what all the fuss is about.

I glance at Sandy's vacant bed. She must be in the kitchen. Outside the window stands a tall tree laden with hanging basket nests and a flock of canary-yellow-and-black birds returning home for the evening.

I have no idea what time it is. The pastel sky contrasts with the darkening jungle, and the tree's shadows loom over the roof.

I sense a presence watching me. My eyes scan the screened window, and beyond the doorway, a short athletically built indigenous man with glossy raven hair approaches the casita. A boyish-looking man accompanies him. As they near the door the older one calls out in Spanish, "Hi, I am here for the consultation."

"Hi," I respond while kicking my feet into my flip-flops. I follow him down the steps. He leads us over to a circular palm-frond covered table immediately behind the row of casitas. Both men sit opposite me, looking at me expectantly.

I look over at the older one who naturally carries an air of authority. I notice his aquiline nose and regal cheekbones. His Rainbow Obsidian eyes fall into mine.

I have seen those eyes before. But where?

I flash quickly through my memories; unable to locate those eyes, I wrench away from his gaze and look down at the wavy grain in the wooden table.

He introduces himself, "My name is Ricardo. I will be your *curandero*, your shaman." He pauses and adds, "I am referred to as Puma." Turning his head slightly I catch his Incan profile. "This is Eduardo. He is the translator if you need his services." He pauses briefly, "And your name is?"

Suddenly, I'm tongue-tied and lose my Spanish. Ricardo, Puma, with flint eyes like the Apache warrior Victoriano, pierces the veil I'm hiding behind. I know he can read me, my every thought. I breathe and pull myself together.

"Georgina."

"Why are you here? What do you want to accomplish?" Puma gets right to the point. Before he's even finished, Eduardo interrupts, translating into English. Except, it's easier for me to understand their Spanish rather than his poor English.

To make my point, I answer back in Spanish to let them both know I understand them just fine. "I get terrible menstrual cramps and get very sick. This has been going on for a long time, and I want to get well. Other than that, I feel good."

"And," remembering, "I am stuck in my life and need change, but I don't know what to do. That's about it." I smile at the small task ahead of us.

Puma nods. "Do you have any questions?" His eyes probe deeply into the black vortices of my pupils.

"No." I don't know what else to say, so I stammer, "Thank you."

We are finished, for now.

"Okay. Where is your friend? I need to talk to her, too."

"I think she is in the dining area talking to Humberto."

"I will go and find her." He swings his legs, pivoting gracefully over the bench and walks away.

Eduardo stays put. Sitting across from me, he starts a conversation in English. I answer him in Spanish. I learn he is studying to be a teacher at the university in Iquitos. He asks what I do, how old I am, and where am I from. I tell him. Then he starts into this speech about what kind of woman he is looking for. *Oh, great!!* Apparently, I am the perfect woman for him. He goes on to sell me on how good we would be together. How he is into equality for women. How he treats women like queens. Blah, blah. I wonder why it always ends up in some pickup situation. Bored. I tell him I am married to get him off my case. But that doesn't deter him. I then tell him I am exhausted from my long journey and I must sleep, now! I get up to leave, and like a sticky shadow, he follows behind me.

I get to the path that leads to my casita. I see Sandy talking to Puma on a nearby bench and wave at her. "Goodbye," I tell Eduardo, hoping he will get the hint and stop following me. He does, and heads off toward the dining area.

The night takes over the jungle, bringing the nocturnal creatures to life.

The insect's vibratory hum replaces the bird's day songs. Their crescendos plateau, announcing that night has officially arrived. Mosquitos emerge hungry from their hiding spots, indicating it's time to dig out the repellent. Sufficiently smelly and protected by OFF! I open *Secrets of Shamanism* by José Stevens, a small paperback I brought along, hoping I would learn about the subject more in depth while working with a real, live shaman.

A few pages into it, Sandy says, "I'm hungry. I wonder what time it is." Neither of us is in the habit of wearing watches. "Maybe we should walk over to see if dinner is ready. They said dinner is at six. I bet it is later than that. It's been dark a while now."

Georgina Lucy Kemm

Using the stub of a plane ticket, I mark my place and toss the book onto my pillow. I stumble around looking for my pack so I can locate my flashlight. The only light is the flame from a small tin kerosene lantern over in the corner. And, Sandy blows out it out on her way out the door.

chapter thirty

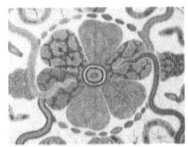

As we descend the steps of the dining hall, a lithe black man with dreads passes by. "*Hola,*" he greets us with a British accent.

Inside, a chestnut-haired European-looking man in his early thirties converses with Humberto's sister, Maria, who seems to be hanging on his every word. His Spanish is mixed with English and Italian. But Maria doesn't seem to have a problem understanding him as she leans across the table as if to hear him better.

By the looks of the mostly empty serving containers, dinner has been ready for a while. Maria rushes off into the kitchen and a few moments later re-emerges with silverware and two plates. She puts them in an empty glass mug and sets the plates in front of Sandy and me. Not far behind her, Juanita saunters out to replenish the bowls with more food. She looks out the corner of her eye at us. I get the impression she is assessing us while she refills the containers on the table. We thank her, and she walks away as if she didn't even hear us.

The European man, Giovanni, is actually Italian. He is staying for ten days. He's been here for a few days already. This is his first experience with ayahuasca. He said he's had a few visions but nothing like he's read about in books. But it has been interesting regardless.

Sandy tells him, "If the ayahuasca is good you should see a lot and go on lots of journeys." She continues, "I've never heard of people not seeing anything. How many ceremonies have you done so far?"

"Just three."

"We were here before, and the ceremonies were super intense," I tell him. "Sandy has done some before at another place, she's more the expert. She will be able to tell us if the ayahuasca is good or not. Right, Sandy?"

"I'm sure it is good, but yeah, I will be able to tell."

We continue our conversation until it feels really late. Maybe it's because I'm exhausted. I ask Giovanni what time it is. It is only eight P.M. So early, I think. There are no lights on anywhere. But with no electricity, everyone goes to bed early.

The three of us turn on our flashlights and follow the silver beams back to our casitas. Giovanni stays in the casita right before ours. We say our goodnights. Looking down on the ground to make sure we don't step on anything, we walk the dirt path to the steps of our hut.

Inside I relight the kerosene lantern. Sandy shines her flashlight into one of her bags and draws out a candle in a tin she brought from home. There is a shelf in the room that is meant for clothing storage, but Sandy and I move it between our beds, creating an altar. She places the candle in the center. Around it, she adds crystals along with some white sage.

On the inside cover of my journal, I remove two cards wrapped in plastic that I bought at the new-age bookstore at home. One is the goddess of the soul and the moon, Ix Chel and the other the Black Madonna. I add my amber citrine crystal and a candle. I then place a necklace of red and black *huaydura* beads with a piranha's jaw Humberto gave me last time and arrange it around the crystals.

"Now it looks like a proper altar," I announce.

She lights the candle. We both get into our beds, unraveling the mosquito net above and tuck the edges securely under the mattress.

"Sweet dreams," I wish her and close my eyes.

chapter thirty-one

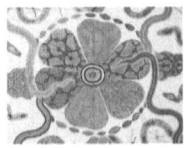

I wake with a start.

I hear a scuttle on the beams overhead.

The creature runs to the vertical pole in the corner. It scratches its way halfway down and lands with a heavy thud right behind my head. I double check the mosquito net, making sure it hasn't untucked itself anywhere, pretending that as long as I am inside the net, I must be safe. I take deep slow breaths, calming my rapidly beating pulse.

"Sandy, did you hear that?"

"Yeah, it must be rats. They come out at night. Try to go back to sleep."

"Okay. I'm putting my earplugs in." I close my eyes and try to fall asleep again.

Now nervous, any little sound awakens me. I hate rats. I have hated rats since junior high school when I read a scary novel called, *The Rats*. Ever since, they have creeped me out. Once in Thailand, I refused to cross a pedestrian walkway over a busy road because there was a huge black ring-tailed rat hissing at the base of the stairs. I chose to take the long way around, venturing several blocks out of the way.

Time seems to pass so slowly when you want to sleep. It feels like the hours spread into days. I try listening to a CD with the sound of breaking waves that usually puts me to sleep. I get up and take my Deep Sleep herbal concoction, waiting patiently for it to kick in. It never does. I can hear

Sandy in the bed next to me breathing butterfly wings. Lucky her.

I don't know what time of the night it is when I hear a weighty pair of boots walk by the end of my bed. I grab my flashlight from out under my pillow and press the button, turning it on.

I don't see anyone.

But I sense a man looking at me.

Squinting in the fuzzy gray light, I still don't see anyone. The heavy boots cross creaking floorboards and walk off into the darkness. It must be a ghost. Although he doesn't feel threatening, now I am really freaked out. My eyes wide open, I lay there beneath my imagined protective mosquito net, the flashlight squeezed in my clammy hands. I hold it atop my chest, in case I have to turn it on quickly. I wish the sun would hurry up.

Eventually, looking out the screened window I see the faint Creamsicle-orange of the morning light. Now, I let myself fall asleep; there is nothing from the night left to scare me. I am safe to sleep, and I let my body sink down into the mattress.

It seems like minutes later that I hear Sandy tread quietly across the room to the shower. She lets out a short shriek as the water, still cold from the night, splashes down on her.

Next door I hear the slam of Giovanni's door. It must be breakfast time. I dress. Put on my flip-flops and sit outside on the step and wait for Sandy to finish getting ready. She opens the door looking gorgeous. She's wearing a new lavender tank top and a pair of earrings and a necklace to match.

I smile at her, "You look beautiful!"

"Well, I like to put on my jewelry. It makes me feel feminine. Are you ready?"

At breakfast, we meet the lanky black guy we saw descending the dining hall steps the night before. He is clad in army greens and eating a whole fish in a bowl. On the side, he's got a cup of liquified oatmeal and a plate of plain, white rice and a cooked banana.

"Hello, I'm Mark," he announces in a cockney London accent.

"I'm Georgina, and this is Sandy," I gesture to my right where Sandy sits.

"I hope we don't get fish soup for breakfast," I say.

"You just bloody might!" Mark chimes in.

"God, I hope not. I haven't been in the jungle long enough to eat like a local. How long have you been here?"

"A couple of months," Mark says, pulling at about two months' worth of wooly beard. "I am doing *dieta*, a special diet. So, I must eat really plain food, but I need a lot of protein, too. That's why I eat fish for breakfast. And lunch. And, for that matter, dinner too!" he says, wrinkling his nose.

"Don't you get sick of the same bland food all the time?" I ask.

"Even if I am not hungry I force myself to eat. I'd stuff into my belly an ocean of fish if I could. I have lost a lot of weight and the gringos who come here comment on how skinny I am." I notice the shoulders of his shirt droop down to mid-deltoid. "But I'm on *dieta*, so I can't help it." He acts annoyed.

"How long are you doing *dieta* for?" Sandy inquires.

"I was planning to do nine months."

Wow! That's a pregnancy.

"But there have been a lot of power games going on, and quite frankly, I am sick of the bullshit, and I might leave." He crosses his bony arms. "Before you came, they would bring me my food to my hut. But they sometimes brought it late or didn't bring it at all. I would have to come to the kitchen and find someone to cook for me. Fucking pisses me off. I paid a lot of money to be here and study plant medicine!!" I can see his blood pressure rising, and images of his eyes popping out like on a spring, spinning uncontrollably, flash through my mind.

Changing the subject, I ask, "Where is your hut?"

"It is the last hut down at the end of the path. You cross over the other bridge," pointing out the window, "and keep walking. You can come and see it if you like."

I am in awe of Mark, living here in the jungle, studying plants. Makes me want to do it, too. But I don't know if I could eat fish soup twice a day!

chapter thirty-two

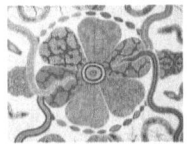

Tonight is our first ceremony.

So today we get breakfast and lunch, but no dinner.

Between meals, Sandy and I decide to take a walk. We ask Maria where is a good place to walk. She recommends that we go out to the road, or rather the sandy footpath, and take a right which would take us the way we came. Or we could go left and walk for many kilometers before we get to a road. Sandy and I decide to take a left in case we want to walk a long way.

From the heavy rain, the path is slick with mud. I abandon my flip-flops and walk barefoot. The sun's heat beats down on me. I'm not used to the temperature and humidity and paddle around awhile in a stream to cool off. We don't pass a single soul on the path and only spot a few huts off to the side.

The jungle, thick with trees and singing birds, forms a protective skin surrounding me. I get lost in my thoughts and walk trancelike. Out of nowhere, I notice a huge, royal-blue butterfly flapping languidly in front of my nose, as if it's leading me somewhere. I follow behind, caught up in the elegance of its flight. Then, finished with me, it flutters off into the trees. I have heard about this butterfly, the Blue Morpho. Sometimes the wings can be the size of a man's hands. I take it as a good sign, perhaps even a message. Butterflies mean transformation. Maybe that is what it came to tell me.

My stomach dictates with a rumble what time it must be, lunchtime. Sandy and I turn around and head back to the center. Going this direction seems much farther. Hungry and hot, we drag our sweaty selves the final part of the walk.

"I'm going to take a shower and try to cool down before lunch," I announce.

"Okay. I want to get something to drink so I'll see you at lunch then."

I approach the casita and notice a couple of young men at the back of the hut.

I walk around and say, "*Hola.*" And they respond with shy "holas" to me. I wonder what they are doing? I see one is carrying a large bucket of water from the rust-colored creek. He passes it to the other guy who climbs up a rickety, stick ladder onto the bathroom roof where he dumps the water in a large tub. It dawns on me that this is how we get our shower water.

I feel a little guilty at enjoying long showers several times a day, deciding to cut down. I realize how spoiled I am. I am used to turning on a tap and having an endless flow of water come out. But here, I can see someone actually goes to a lot of work so I can take a shower.

I'm thinking about fish soup, but we get noodles with onions and tomatoes, accompanied by a cabbage salad, sliced tomatoes, and onions. But the best part is the fresh-squeezed orange juice.

"You better eat a lot. This is your last meal today, and you are going to need all your energy," Mark advises as he extracts fine bones from his bowl.

Sounds ominous. But I don't want to stuff myself; I take regular-sized portions. I look over at Giovanni. He heaped his plate with food and Sandy is taking seconds already.

Puma enters the dining hall and pads quietly across the floor.

He's come from the kitchen, where the employees eat. Today he wears blue plastic horn-rimmed glasses which match his blue plaid polyester shirt. I smile to myself, wondering if he knows how silly he looks in women's glasses. He seats himself at the head of the table, folding and re-folding the corner of the tablecloth like he is nervous about sitting with us. He makes small talk, asking how our lunch was. Then, as if he remembers why he came to the dining room in the first place, Puma turns to Mark and tells him that he will see him back in his casita after lunch. I notice Puma calls him Marcos, the Spanish version of Mark.

Puma jumps up from the table and says, "*Chao*, goodbye." He puts on his blue rubber boots parked at the door and leaves.

Mark has been studying with Puma for only three weeks. The other shaman Mark worked with previously left. He said he felt like he wasted a lot of time with the other shaman. Mark thought that he didn't want to teach him anything and he was playing games with him. Or the shaman's wife would come along, and he would spend most of his time doing healings on her and not teaching. Mark felt that the shaman didn't want to share his knowledge with others. He hadn't taught him any *icaros*, songs during ceremonies. Before he left, he started sharing the icaros and plant medicine. Mark thought that this shaman was chased out of the center by other shamans in the area who also didn't want knowledge shared. So, Mark was pissed off by that. He said that he's learned more in the past several weeks from Puma than his previous months. But he still doesn't trust any of them.

After sharing this information, Mark announces he will see us later. He puts on his rubber boots, and clomping down the steps, he crosses the bridge and vanishes into the jungle.

I'm ready for a nap and walk back to the casita. I leave the door open to circulate the air and lie down in the hammock. I guess I must have fallen asleep because I wake up a while later to see Sandy asleep on her bed. I don't remember her coming into the room.

The lack of sleep must be catching up with me.

chapter thirty-three

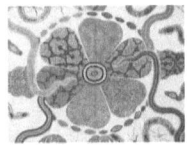

D aydreaming and gently swinging in the hammock I hear a "Whu who" from down the path.

It's Puma approaching the hut. "*Hola.*"

"*Hola*," I reply. This wakes Sandy up.

"Can I come in?" Puma asks.

"Yes, of course! Come in." I leap off the bed and open the screen door.

He drops his flip-flops on the top step before entering. He lingers inside the doorway.

"I came to tell you that at four o'clock, you will have a mud bath."

We both respond, "Okay."

Then Sandy asks, "Where?"

"Down by the creek, farther down the path," Puma replies, pointing towards the dense overgrowth.

"Can you come and get us?" I ask him. "We don't have a clock." Adding, "What time is it now?"

"It is two o'clock." Looking at his bulky silver watch and giving the face a couple of taps, "I will be here at four on the dot. Chao!" He turns on his heel and walks back down the path.

Sure enough, Puma arrives precisely at four. Towels draped over our shoulders, we cross the bridge over the stream and head into the shadowy woods. Sunlight streams through the tall trees looming high above, creating a tunnel-like canopy over the walking trail. The trail splits, and we take the left fork. Puma mentions that the right fork leads to the casitas where he and Marcos live.

We reach a cleared area. The brick-red water winds its way like a shepherd's crook and passes under a fallen log. Puma digs into the bank extracting a handful of ash-colored mud. He does this several times until he has enough of the clay mixture in a large handmade earthenware pot. He then scoops out a few handfuls of water and blends the mud and water together to make a smooth paste. Placing the pot on the ground in an orb-like patch of sunshine, he closes his eyes, resting his hands over the pot, giving the mud a blessing.

I expect to apply the mud ourselves but then Puma pipes up, "Who wants to go first?"

Feeling self-conscious that a strange man would be touching me, "Why don't you go first?" I offer.

"Sure," she says and faces Puma, "Where do you want me to stand?"

"Over here in the sunshine." He points in front of him. "You need to take off your top so it won't get muddy. You can put it there on the bench."

Doing so, she gives me a look that says, "What the hell!!"

I stand watching and slapping the mosquitos nibbling my pale skin. Puma extracts two handfuls of mud. With eyes closed, he rubs the gray substance in circular motions over Sandy's diminutive bosom. Then he scoops more and applies it carefully to her face, hair, and neck. He covers the rest of her body with mud. When she is completely covered he instructs her to go and stand in a large patch of sunshine to let it dry.

My turn.

I quickly take off my bikini top and toss it onto the bench.

I walk over to the sunshine where Puma waits ready with a handful of mud. Standing before him I watch his closed eyes as he rubs mud onto my abdomen stopping at the seam of my bikini bottoms. He reaches for more and slowly applies the slippery stuff to the tops of my legs, then to the inside of my thighs and glides down around my ankles. With my legs sufficiently covered, he scoops more mud from the pot and applies it on my upper chest. His hands move swiftly around the underside curve of my breasts. Cupping them in his hands, he lifts them gently upward as he continues to apply the smooth, cool mud.

Although Puma maintains the guise of professional seriousness, I have my suspicions that this mud bath is not solely for medicinal purposes. I have the sneaky feeling that he is probably enjoying this mud bath as much as I am pretending not too.

Finishing, he takes more mud and paints my face and neck. With a couple of handfuls, he covers my hair and directs me to where Sandy is baking in the hot sun. I feel the mud stiffening, and I keep my arms away from my body to help speed up the drying process.

At least the mosquitos can't bite through all this mud. But my face starts to tighten as the mud slowly dries in the warm sun. I rotate my body so my backside can also dry. I look over my shoulder at Puma. He is up to his knees in water, washing the caked mud out of the clay pot at the bend in the creek where it creates a small pool. Glancing over, he tells Sandy she looks dry enough to wash off. She walks over to the pool and gets in the water. She emerges shiny in the sunlight and walks over to the bench to put on her top and sit down to dry.

I close my eyes and bask in the warmth of the sun a little longer. When I feel sufficiently dry, I slide into the water with my back to both of them. The mud sticks, and it takes some effort to scrub off. I have difficulty with my hair, and Puma asks if I need help. He walks over, and I drop into the water, so my body is not visible to him. Leaning back he gently swishes my hair in the creek to loosen the mud. Satisfied that it is clean enough, I pull my head up and look at him. He looks at my ears and rubs a thumb over them removing the mud residue. He moves away from the bank, so I have space to climb out.

Quickly, as to appear unnoticed, I trot to the bench to put my bikini top back on. When I sit down, I notice a scarlet rash erupting over my legs and arms. It starts to feel itchy.

"Why am I getting a rash?" I ask Puma.

"The mud pulls toxins out of the body."

I look over at Sandy, but her skin looks perfectly normal. "You're not itchy, are you?"

"No, only where the mosquitos bit me. My skin just feels like a raisin." She comments. "Are you ready to go back?"

"Yeah, I guess so. The mosquitos are annoying me."

We tell Puma that we are ready to go.

"Let's go!" And he swings the heavy clay pot onto his shoulder like it's an empty paper bag and leads us back down the path.

Giovanni sees us from his screen window.

"Hey, girls. Where have you been?"

We walk over to his door, and he let us in.

"We just had a mud bath," I report. Noticing his journal on his bed, I ask, "What are you doing?"

"I'm listening to some music and preparing myself for the ceremony tonight." He reaches for a small digital tape recorder, "I am going to ask Puma if I can tape the ceremony. I want to put some of the icaros onto my blog along with some of my experiences in the ceremonies."

"That is a great idea," Sandy says. "I also brought along a tape recorder. I like to listen to the icaros at home. It helps keep me more in the spirit world because once I get home, I get caught up in the rat race."

"Well, I am going to go and rest and distract myself from my hunger. See you!" I tell them, walking toward the door.

"Wait! I'm coming with you," says Sandy, following right behind me.

Once back in our room, I lie down on my bed, leaving the hammock for Sandy. My rash seems to have calmed down, and my skin feels silky to touch.

"What did you think about the mud bath? Do you think that Puma was having fun with us? I mean rubbing mud over us like he did?" I ask.

"I have never taken off my bathing suit for a mud bath. Before we did it ourselves, put the mud on. It was kind of odd. But it felt harmless enough to me."

I don't know. It isn't sitting right with me, but I let it go.

chapter thirty-four

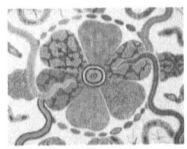

I'm dressed in long pants, wool socks, and a long-sleeved button-up shirt.

I don't want to chance any mosquitoes sucking my blood during the ceremony.

I also have a sweater in case I get cold. I hug everything close to my chest and slide into my shoes. Somberly, we walk single file to the ceremonial *maloca*.

We enter, adding our shoes to the collection of shoes amassed inside the doorway. The room is barely lit, with one kerosene lantern placed on the floor in front of Puma. I notice a worn black leather Bible next to his cigarettes and lighter. A half coconut shell sits upside down next to a recycled water bottle containing the dark brown liquid. A palm frond rattle rests near a pair of *maracas* with white shells dangling from the handle.

I choose a protective spot between Giovanni and Sandy. I arrange my yoga mat and pillow against the wall. I place my flashlight within arm's reach next to my water bottle. A roll of toilet paper sits between two, large plastic basins; one for each of us.

Across the room, Marcos smokes what looks like homemade, roll-your-own cigarettes. He calls them *mapacho*; wild black tobacco.

Puma addresses Marcos, "Tonight practice your icaros, the magic songs. You need to practice with people around you if you want to be a *maestro,* and be Master of the medicine."

"But I don't remember them all," he complains.

"You will remember the melody, it'll come to you, and that's the most important part."

Then Puma tosses his nearly finished cigarette. Sizzling, it hits the water in the bottom of the basin. As if for reassurance, he reaches out to touch his Bible, making sure it is nearby. He then grabs the bottle containing the dark, chocolaty-looking substance, ayahuasca. He tips it back and forth slowly, mixing the thick part on the bottom with the watery, upper liquid. Carefully, he unscrews the plastic cap and a rush of gassy air escapes. He brings the bottle up to his lips, quietly whistling a tune into the bottle. He takes the coconut cup and pours some of the liquid into it and calls Marcos over. Marcos kneels and accepts the cup. He holds it for a moment and tips it quickly into his mouth. He gives a quick shudder and returns to his place against the wall. Puma invites Humberto to drink the medicine, but he declines. Next, Giovanni, then Sandy, and finally it is my turn.

On my knees, I take the half-full cup.

As I draw it closer to my face, a smell like no other rams my senses.

I tip the cup back quickly, and in two gulps the viscous fluid is down. I get up quickly and reach for my water bottle to rinse out the acrid residue in my mouth.

Marcos calls from across the room, "Don't drink the water," he reminds me. "It dilutes the ayahuasca in your stomach."

I fill my mouth and swish around the water and spit into the bucket. But still, the potency lingers, causing me to screw up my face. How awful! The taste gets worse every time. A shudder runs through my body, I have never tasted anything quite so horrible.

The quiet room hums with the chorus of the insects outside. We wait for the effects of the ayahuasca to kick in. A while later, Puma blows out the light. We sit with eyes closed, silent in the darkness.

The sound of the metallic wheel of Puma's lighter spin as he ignites a cigarette. Smoke wafts my direction, escaping through the window's mesh above my head. It feels like we have been waiting a long time for the ayahuasca to take effect. I am not feeling anything, only gassy and a little tired.

Puma rises to his feet and walks to the center of the room. He commences with a prayer, "*Dios bendiga...*" He asks for protection and healing. When he finishes, he takes his place on the floor again, and we wait some more. Eventually, he gets up and sings an icaro. Still feeling nothing, I see some dark shapes moving faintly before me. I can't make out what they are.

I lean over to Sandy, "I am not feeling anything are you?"

"No," she growls. "I think this is bad ayahuasca. We should be really feeling it by now."

I don't know how much time has passed, it feels like a long time, when Sandy blurts out, "We don't feel anything. All I feel is tired."

"It is because it is your first time," Puma tells us.

"It's not my first time and my first time I felt and saw a lot. We paid a lot of money to be here, and we didn't pay for crap ayahuasca," she says hotly.

"Maybe you didn't diet long enough before you got here."

"Yes, we did!! For two weeks, just like I did before. I am not sitting around in here with nothing happening. I am tired, and I am going to bed." She gathers her things together. I copy her. She stomps over to her shoes with me following right behind her.

Back in our hut, she fumes, "I can't believe they gave us that shit! Poor Giovanni has put up with this because he doesn't know any better. And no wonder Marcos is pissed with crap like that. I'm surprised he didn't leave a long time ago. Tomorrow I am going to talk to Humberto. At Jon's we got to participate in making the brew. I just can't believe it!!"

I don't know what to say but I feel like there has been a major injustice committed.

I am hungry and ask Sandy for a bag of rice cakes. She pulls one out of the bottom of the pack and rips open the plastic and hands me one.

Sitting silent and cross-legged on our beds, we crunch on the dry, hard cakes.

chapter thirty-five

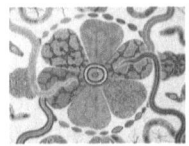

Next morning, Sandy demands to talk to Humberto. After breakfast, Humberto, Julio, Puma and a few employees join us around the table. Humberto is still making up reasons why the ayahuasca didn't have any effect when Sandy chimes in:

"You shouldn't be using bad ayahuasca. When I was at another healing center, every ceremony was powerful with lots of visions. We also got to help prepare it and say prayers over the brew as it was cooking. We put our intentions into it, and it was a very intense healing experience." She takes a breath, then continues through tears, "We paid a lot of money to get here. Just because we are gringos doesn't mean we are rich. I have three daughters. I am a single mom, and it cost me a lot to get here. I don't have money to throw away. We came here to heal. We came here because we need help. We didn't come for a good time! We live in a country that is very sick. It is sick spiritually, and we get sick living like that!"

Her eyes are brimming with tears and I feel a lump forming in my throat from watching her in emotional anguish. I glance around at the others, and they appear distraught by her words.

Humberto pipes up, "You can make your own brew. We can start after this conversation." He continues magnanimously, "I understand that you came here to heal, and if there is anything I can do to help you, please let us know."

"Thank you." She sniffles showing him a small smile.

"Okay. Puma, take them out the fire pit and get started on preparing the ayahuasca," dictates Humberto.

Accompanied by a few workers, we walk over to the fire pit located beneath an open framed structure with the typical palm roof. A couple of hammocks drape lazily between support poles. The workers wrestle with three large logs. Pushed together, they create a small pyramid space to place the ayahuasca pot.

Puma is on his hands and knees, digging through rotting brown leaves, searching for a hidden treasure. He finds what he is looking for; what looks like nothing more than a pile of sticks to me. Extracting the branches from their hiding spot he moves them out of the sun into the shade of the palm-roofed hut. Leaning a branch against a log, he takes a club like stick and pounds it until it shreds apart like stringy brisket. This he tells me is the vine of the ayahuasca. Giovanni, Sandy and I offer to help smash the branches, since it looks like hard work. My arms tire quickly, and I sit down and watch as they finish.

With an ample pile of shredded vine, Puma instructs one of his helpers to bring a large cauldron over near the fire. He covers the bottom of the pot with ayahuasca. Then he reaches into a large sack and tosses in eye-shaped green leaves. This is the *chacruna*. It is responsible for the visions during the ceremony. We each grab handfuls of leaves, throwing them on top of the vine. We layer them like lasagne, adding more stringy vine and leaves until the pot is full. They then hoist it onto the pyramid of burning logs and add water, covering the mixture of vine and leaves. Puma tells us it takes many hours and won't be ready until late in the afternoon. He walks over to a hammock, where he informs us he will sit and watch the brew cooking for a while.

chapter thirty-six

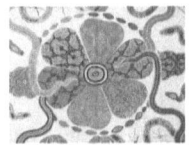

Feeling more confident, we decide to go for a walk.
We choose to walk to a lake that is near the village we passed on our way here. Eduardo decides to accompany us. *Oh, no*! I fear he is going to be annoyingly flirty again. Maria also joins us, even though we said we would be okay by ourselves.

We, three women, walk side by side across the white powdery path. Eduardo saunters a few paces behind, bringing up the rear.

Maria is very chatty. She tells us about her life. She has two kids, a boy, and a girl. Lupe, whom we already have met. She is officially married, but her husband left her for another woman. We asked her why she didn't get divorced. It costs too much money to get a lawyer, she says. Sometimes the husband takes her son for weeks, who has him now, and she must plead to get him back. She makes money from *artesanía*, handicrafts she makes and sells, and also from helping at the center. She made the bedspreads in our rooms and some that hang in the dining hall.

Her whole family came from farther south, near Pucallpa. Maria doesn't elaborate and quickly glosses over the tragedy that brought them to this place. Her grandfather owned the land where the center now sits. When they first arrived in Iquitos, they were terribly poor. Their only income was from the *artesanía* they managed to sell on the street to tourists. Some days they didn't make any money at all.

Her grandfather was a *curandero*, a traditional healer. Somehow a gringo had heard about him. This gringo was writing a book on altered realities and plant medicine and had done some ceremonies with her grandfather. The gringo so enjoyed his experience with Maria's grandfather that he wanted to donate money and open a healing center. Humberto got involved because he would be able to be on site and organize the workers and materials.

And that is how the family ended up at the center.

I forgot about Eduardo trotting behind us like an obedient puppy, when he pipes up that he must stop at this hut. Pointing to the right, he said he would catch up with us later. I ask Maria what he's doing, and she said he was probably going to the bathroom, so we continued off toward the lake.

At the lake, Sandy and I take off capris and t-shirts and place them on the wooden dock. Maria jumps right in, clothes and all. I double check with Maria and make sure there aren't any piranhas or those small fish that crawl up your urethra. Laughing, she assures me no, because this is a lake and not a river. We swim around the dock made of small logs roped together. On top of the bank, young children stand laughing and pointing at us. They aren't used to pale-skinned women making a spectacle of themselves. We emerge from the water and sit for a while, drying our skin in the sunshine. A couple of the braver kids climb like mountain goats down the slippery bank to get a better look. We wave and say hello and attempt to strike up a conversation. Apparently, this is very funny, and they giggle, running back up the hill to safety.

On the walk back to the center Maria continues chatting away. She tells us about female circumcision that the Shipibo tribe practices. Horrified, I ask her if that still goes on. She assures me that it doesn't, it stopped with her mother's generation. I share with her that in parts of Africa they still do that even though it is illegal and that many girls die. I tell her about my friend in Kenya who goes to remote villages during circumcision season and rescues girls about to be circumcised. "If a girl is circumcised, her father will get a better bride price for her," I say. "So, he will get more cows or goats which adds to his value, not hers. That is why it is still popular. Plus, her shame of not honoring her father encourages the girls to continue the practice. The girls that are not yet circumcised wear a certain color beaded belt. The circumcised girls have a different styled belt that they proudly wear, flaunting their new status."

Maria quickly changes the subject, leaving me a little suspicious that maybe the practice of female circumcision still exists here.

This got me thinking back to the mud bath and how I didn't object or speak up. And, how I let it go as "normal." Even though as I'm speaking about it, it's not normal. I know that. Sometimes I still feel like a child, the little girl with no voice to talk about all the things that don't feel right. Who would believe me? So why bother? I'll just keep the truth about what I know locked inside, what I've experienced, for fear of being told I'm lying. And, if you are told you're a liar often enough, then you won't even know your own truth.

I don't know what the truth is anymore. When I was a child, adults would say one thing. Yet on the inside, what felt true didn't match up. So, I chose to believe the adult, the one with power, for they must certainly know what's true, what's right and wrong. No? I'm sure this is how people go crazy and schizophrenic; when it's impossible to believe the truth they're left believing the lies and illusions. No wonder I'm in a schizoid knot inside.

I think this is the definition of powerlessness, relying on someone else's opinion. Power must be when you are your own resource for truth and guidance. What about the saying "He is powerful?" What makes him powerful? It's not that he is powerful but that you give him power over you by thinking he knows best for you, like the government or teachers or preachers. Who decided they know best? Because we turn everyone into our mother or father and God and think we depend on them for our survival. Even as an adult. That is why I lose my voice, because I think I will die if I offend or contradict what they think is true.

Anyway, back to the present, who thought female circumcision was a brilliant idea?

Probably not a woman.

As we enter the grounds of the center, I notice we have lost Eduardo way back near Jan Chama. I figure he already made it back. Sandy goes with Maria and Lupe to the dining hall, and I walk down the narrow path back to our casita. I take a quick shower and change into something less sweaty.

I'm curious to see how the ayahuasca is coming along and head over to the *palapa* where the brewing is taking place. I get there as Puma and one of the workers grab a metal handle on each side of the huge pot. They remove it from the fire, setting it carefully on the soil.

"Do you want to see it?" Puma asks me.

I walk over as he lifts the lid off with a stick, revealing the same intense smell that is becoming so familiar. I step back whipping my head away, "Aghh!"

They both laugh at me.

"I will reduce it down. It should be ready for tonight's ceremony," Puma tells me.

A quick wave of panic rushes through me in anticipation of the impending ceremony.

"Chao. I'm going to the kitchen." I leave them to their brewing.

Sandy and Maria sit at the table stringing tiny beads onto a thin silver sewing needle. Sandy is teaching Maria how to make beaded earrings.

I sit down in front of a large plate of cut up mango and scoop some into a bowl.

I hear the faint sound of the moto-taxi's engine putter as it drives up to the healing center's entrance. A few moments later and my second bowl of mango, Humberto pushes back the screen door and allows a platinum-haired man to pass in front of him.

"Hello," he says in a tired, British accent.

Humberto dashes off to the kitchen, re-emerging with another plate. Setting it down, he introduces this James Bond look-alike as, Gavin. But the way Humberto pronounces the "v" makes it sound more like Gabin. We do a round of introductions as Gavin politely nods his head.

"You are just in time for ceremony," Sandy says, looking over the rim of her eye-glasses. "I hope you've been doing your dieta."

"Dieta?"

"You know, your diet restrictions."

"Oh yes! And I haven't eaten it thirty hours. My plane was delayed and had to circle back to Spain. I guess the weather was too stormy to land," he continues, "I don't eat airplane food or the food at the airports. So, really, I've been fasting on water."

"Wow!" Is all I can say before pushing the bowl of juicy mango closer to him.

I can share, even though I'm well aware that this will be my last meal today.

Tonight's ceremony starts in just over four hours.

chapter thirty-seven

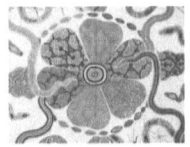

Robotic insects pull with needles and daggers, loosening and extracting cemented patterns.

The insects in my vision represent beliefs and thought forms epoxied inside my body and mind. They keep my body stuck, not fluid and flexible. And my mind is an ancient ruin held up by the past. I think this is normal, but, it's not part of who I am. They hold me in a restrictive mold.

My thoughts drag me back to early in the day. Woven into a fibrous web where I am the center. I see myself enmeshed in plasmic light fibers that reach inside my womb and out into the universe at the same time. *Where am I?*

A voice spans across the vast pitch-black I'm tumbling through. *We want to say, when you abandon yourself and give yourself away to others, to anything outside yourself, you abandon the feminine principle within you – the innate state of being open and free and full of creating and mastering your own life and world. When you are not home in your body, or someone else's energy, thoughts, wishes, and demands have taken residence within, the feminine is locked up in a dark corner, hiding out, waiting for her moment to be reclaimed. Usually, it isn't and wreaks havoc in life because although she isn't seen or let out of hiding, her shadow will dominate the life. As in your story, letting others decide for you and make decisions on your behalf takes the feminine voice away and she shows up in the area of self-importance, begging to be seen, by the males, the masculine, so she can have her space and her words. If a woman acts dominating or in a masculine, patriarchal way, the feminine within won't overtly demand to be seen but the shadow will acquiesce to be seen, and the person will be seen as weak and a doormat. If the feminine principle isn't owned within the body by bringing the body into an awakened and enlivened state within her domain, she cannot function correctly. Understand, the feminine principle can't be done in the mind with the intellect. She can only be known through the body, primarily the womb space and in the neural network pathways that reach out to the center of the galaxy to retrieve information unknown by the intellect. Her perception grows with this deepening connection to her womb and the network inside and outside must be given priority to serve its function. Because of this capacity to know the unknown and unknowable, because there is no basis for it in this particular reality and no box that it can fit into, she is looked upon as a witch, evil or just plain weird.*

The body has the answers and can be fully trusted when she is open to receiving in this way. Women are taught that it is nobler to give than to receive, to sacrifice themselves for their man and families, leaving them a shell, empty of energy and feeling their innate power for it has all been externalized and given away to the dictates of the culture. The enslavement of women is not only in the past or distant cultures but in your very own "advanced" western culture where you are taught to sacrifice for the greater good while not realizing that your vessel IS the greater good and the connection to the answers and resources for the culture. Honoring the natural cyclical tides of the womb as an aspect of nature and working with the internal rhythms, that is the nature of the feminine. Not by subduing her and taming her into what is suitable, pleasing and most logical to function on a linear trajectory to accomplish the most in the least amount of time. Fighting with your own nature and Mother Nature will always cause a challenge, and you will lose. If you fight the feminine, you will lose. At some point, she will come forth like a flaming dragon and burn clear all that holds her down and blocks her way. The wrath is greater than any hurricane or earthquake you can experience. It will lead you to total annihilation of the self. You will have nothing to do, but quite literally, you will die. The archetypes, the story and themes of the human race are locked within the feminine pole and wait for their opportunity to emerge. It is a story written before you got here that leads you like breadcrumbs on the journey out of the human predicament into the divine being you really are. The human suit helps you drive around the planet as your journey leads you out of this world. The feminine isn't so much about being female, although women have the natural, built-in capacity to lead this direction because of their womb's design. A man can learn to awaken and operate from this area of his body, as well. Soon, in the next generations, males will be born with this capacity, too, and will be seen by the dying ones as odd and sensitive because their perceptive abilities are unconceivable. Yet to a woman who owns and celebrates this part of her body, this will be a welcoming hope for the future, of the Earth Mother and those coming beings. The relic male idea and limitation will die out, and the suffering will vanish with it. To bring the feminine back online and in charge, she must perceive herself much larger and of greater use than that of her biological imperative. Her body doesn't need to be used as the vessel for a man to have his seed and DNA linger on the earth longer. She can use her body as a being of per-

ception to guide and lead her in a direction of wholeness instead of fractionalizing and compartmentalizing into small boxes of convenience.

The voice has been talking for a very long time.

I get bogged down, trying to comprehend the words. It seems I am receiving the information through the light fibers as the frequency transmits directly into my body. I am highly uncomfortable, like I'm itching from the inside out.

I call upon my Eagle to lift me out of my body. We fuse together until I am the Eagle and I can feel my feathers slice through the air. Soaring above my anguish, I can now see the larger perspective. Ayahuasca is releasing me of those patterns that have glued me to a life that isn't mine. Yet, I needed to have lived these cemented thought forms and live in small boxes to taste its opposite, freedom.

With this new view on my life, I can handle more, and I swoop back in and let the insectoids resume their surgery.

After the ceremony, Sandy and Giovanni take a walk.

So tired, all I need is a cane to help me weave and wobble down the sandy path back to the hut. Once back in the hut, I notice my body and my shriveled apple-doll face. Deep crevices wrinkle my cheeks. *Who am I?* Inside my head, a scratchy wool-voice announces that I am, and she is a Cherokee medicine woman. She has come to help me remember who I am. I have shape-shifted into her old, yet vibrant body. My blanket wrapped around my shoulders, I dance around the room singing. My hair, no longer blonde, appears white. On the far side of the narrow creek, I hear leaves rustling and the clippity-cloppity of hooves crossing the log bridge. They stop beneath my window. I pause my song and walk to the window and see who is there. Looking out, I see a man atop a stag's body. A Pan Spirit, joined by many jungle faeries, of all shapes and sizes have come to hear me sing. I resume singing, pulling my heart and third-eye out through my voice. When I finish singing, Pan turns around, clippity-clops cross the bridge. And the other beings disperse into the jungle. A lightness in the body and heart has come with remembering who I am. And, I'm overwhelmed with love and support from so many beings.

In the morning, I sit outside on the bench next to the creek while I wait for Sandy. I get the feeling I am being watched from the jungle's edge. I look behind me and notice branches bending and a handful of rogue leaves falling. Turning around, I see piles of glossy brown Raisinette-sized poops scattered around the plank bench.

A stream of endless painful memories floods out of my thighs, hip flexors, and abdomen.

A hard knot behind my belly button doesn't soften until I probe and prod it with my fingers. Hiding within the knot, I see a lemon-lime colored creature clinging to the backside of my navel, not wanting to release its grip. When it finally breaks loose, I purge, and a deafening shriek fills my ears.

After all the physical sensations ebb and the *mareación*, the intoxicating effects, of the ayahuasca calms down, I feel the Cherokee grandmother on my right side comforting me, enveloping me in her heavy blanket. My persona shifts to adopt her energy and I become again, an old woman.

I reach out in front, patting the ground until I stumble upon a *mapacho*. I pick it up and with shaking hands, light the end. I inhale deeply. With peaceful satisfaction I hold it in my crooked old fingers, smiling at it like I would an old friend. She says smoking would help me remember who I am. I don't see how that would work and it doesn't really matter. I am content as I am.

An owl slices silently through the darkness, landing gracefully on my left shoulder. The owl tells me that she will impart wisdom, especially in the dream state. The old grandmother says the owl is an aspect of me, but I can accept the information better if I think it is separate from me. The problem, she says, is that I don't take responsibility for my own power and instead trust those I think are more powerful to guide me. This will have to stop, she says. *You can no longer barter your energy for insights that aren't for you.*

The following morning, I pass Giovanni sitting with Gavin on the wooden bench next to the white sandy path.

"What were you screaming about in the ceremony?" Giovanni asks.

Confused. "I wasn't screaming." I'm sure I'd remember something like that.

"Was I screaming?" I ask for confirmation from Gavin who nods his head, yes. I was sure that I was the only one hearing the screaming inside my head.

Giovani reaches in the side pocket of his cargo pants and pulls out the tape recorder he uses to record the icaros. I sidle up next to him as he switches on the tape recorder. I hear a gut-wrenching purging sound then suddenly out comes this deep guttural scream that sounds like it comes from the bowels of the earth. I look over at him. I can't believe that is me!

"That doesn't even sound like me!" I tell them. "All I remember is a demon, sticky and yellowish-green, exiting my body, hanging on for dear life." Giovanni rewinds the recording and plays it one more time.

"Yes, that was you." He smiles kindly at me.

"Better out than in!" Gavin chimes in.

Suddenly feeling an incredible urge to lie down, I excuse myself and walk back to the casita. I crawl onto my bed and lay down. Tears leak out the corners of my eye, tickling my hairline. I wipe them away with my hand as I wonder about being possessed by a demon. I don't know what else to call this situation. I wonder if it was this creature that ran my life, not me. *Who is me?* I can't trust anything about me right now. I've been possessed for how many years? Probably my whole life. I begin to ponder what a demon is. How does it get there in the first place?

I remember a terrifying story I read in grade eight about this little boy who became possessed by a devil demon. He got this way because his older sister played with an Ouija board, and she opened a crack in reality that allowed a spirit to enter. Because the boy was young and couldn't defend himself, this is where the demon took hold.

Reviewing my life, I could relate to that feeling as a child: how could I defend myself? I trusted the adults around me to take care of me, to protect me. Some of them were terrible at it. How had this demon snuck in? I thought about this some more. Maybe the demon didn't sneak in. Maybe I created it; this thought caused a shudder throughout my body. Why would I create this slimy creature? It was as if what was an unbearable and terrifying thought or experience that I couldn't cope with and I had no idea what to do with it, so I put it down there behind my belly button, out of the way. The idea is awful; that I created this creature and then hid it away, until last night.

With the demon gone, I feel lost, a deep cavern of emptiness inside.

Who I thought was me is now gone.

I don't know what this will mean. I don't know who I will be now. I roll over on my side to face the wall and hug my knees close to my chest. I let the tears slip over the bridge of my nose onto my pillow until no more flow from the well of sadness.

This morning, I sleep past the change of guard when the night creatures give way to the bird's songs. I wake up lighter and still a little tired. Tightness emanates from my belly as if a scab is beginning to form over a wound.

I wrangle the edge of mosquito net into a knot and toss it upward where it stays on the first try. Swinging my feet off the side of the bed, I sit a moment and get my bearings.

I feel as though I am looking through a long winding tunnel that ventures out into the middle of the universe. Time and space have become melded into one moment; the past and the future do not exist. I have lost the linear path my life took before I came to Peru. Things I believed to be a myth now seem part of my reality. I am forced to expand my mind, my way of being. I shake my head, I don't understand. My only truth is what I feel.

Maybe, sometime later I will make some sense of it all.

chapter thirty-eight

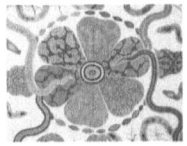

I'm either in a ceremony, preparing, or resting up for the next one.

In the darkness on the maloca floor, I feel overwhelmed suddenly with a love within me that I have never felt before.

I feel the trees leaning into me like grandparents embracing a grandchild. I feel the insects rejoice in symphony that I am back, that I have returned to life. All creatures from the jungle sing how much they love me. Everything and everyone loves me! I sense everything in the entire universe is here to love and support me. I feel so happy for the first time in my life. I feel like I belong. I feel like shouting at the top of my lungs, "I belong! I belong, and everything loves me!" Right now, I feel connected to everything. And from this moment, I really KNOW from the bottom of my heart, that God exists, in me, in absolutely everything.

I thought about all the times I was so mad at God for leaving me on this planet, all by myself. I had been so angry, thinking I had been abandoned and just dropped off to live with humans who had lost touch with how to love and really communicate. Right now, I sort of feel sorry for them and how hopeless they appear to me and maybe that's how they feel about themselves.

I could never understand why people would pray to God for things they wanted and waste their time at church on Sunday. It never made sense to me that God lived in a church. I became especially disillusioned with the whole concept of God when it became intertwined with church and religion. My parents wanted me to attend confirmation classes. I didn't want to, because it took up my valuable time. Plus, there was the homework. We had to study and take tests, and if we didn't have a high enough grade, we would have to retake it. I decided this whole thing was bullshit, and I refused to retake a test I hadn't passed. Also, I didn't respect the preacher. He was squatty and wore a brown robe with a cord for a belt, and he reminded me of Friar Tuck. Because I never got confirmed, I had to sit on the bench while everyone else got to go and eat that little white cracker and drink the grape juice. I felt ostracized.

One time, in the basement of the church. I ate some of those crackers. They stuck to the roof of my mouth worse than peanut butter does. I had to drink a couple of the tiny glasses full of grape juice to help swallow what had turned into a gluey paste. At first, I thought I might get struck down by lightning. Nothing happened, no lightning. And, no angels appeared either. I became even more skeptical and realized the whole thing was a hoax.

From then on I stopped believing in God. But what I was feeling right now, I put the name of God on. It was an all-inclusive love that I never felt inside a church or with people who were religious. Here I was out in the jungle with the bugs knowing for sure that God exists. I think I prefer Great Love, or Source, the All or anything that can describe this feeling instead of a concept. I bet this is what all those people are looking for, in all the wrong places.

I read somewhere that all our problems began when we separated ourselves from the Great Love because we were like teenagers who think they always know better. The famous Fall. And that we project everything outside ourselves so we actually can see ourselves. But, we forgot we are always looking at ourselves, and a split between subject and object began. This even created a division in our brain, giving us the right brain and the left brain.

I realize that ayahuasca bridges the two parts into one again.

The information that rushes into my rational brain is practically blowing my circuits. I can't handle all the images and feelings rushing in, and I don't have any way to control the flow. Good thing I'm not at home where people would think me certifiably crazy.

Until this last ceremony, I swore every one of them would be my last.

Sound asleep, something startles me awake.

I breathe very softly so whatever it is won't notice I'm awake. My eyes strain, peering into the darkness for the small, light feet I hear crossing the creaking wooden floorboards. The sound nears the left side of my bed and stops. Someone is watching me. I peer harder through my mosquito net out into the darkness. I still see no one. My heart beat slows, and my breathing deepens. For some reason, I don't feel afraid. This is the second ghost that has come to visit me here. The first one had heavy footsteps like he was wearing clunky work boots. He was also curious. He stopped at the end of my bed, watched me for a few moments and kept on walking. This one feels benign.

A short while later the weightless footsteps cross the room and disappear into thin air.

Completely awake, I turn my face to one side, watching Sandy sleeping. She hasn't stirred and didn't notice the footsteps. I look at her more intently. She looks different. I squint my eyes, figuring out what has changed about her. My eyes play tricks on me, she looks to me like a black woman. Her features are African, and her hair appears like a peroxide job gone wrong on dark hair. Her orange hair looks like it has been set in rollers; loose big rolls of curls cover her head.

I laugh to myself.

It must be the ayahuasca, seeing and hearing things that I normally can't see with ordinary eyes!

chapter thirty-nine

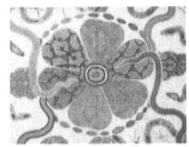

Lying on my bed, I close my eyes and listen to the urgent pitter-patter of rain dancing around on the palm leaves. The cat jumps up to join me for a nap, and its monotonous purring lulls me to sleep.

A knock at the door awakens me. I listen again to make sure I really heard it; that it wasn't in my dream or some other reality. Ratta tat tat. Puma's signature knock. Sandy looks over sleepily.

"I can get it. I think it's Puma." I swing my legs off the side of the bed and drop the cat onto Sandy's bed. I open the door and invite him in. He sits on the corner of Sandy's bed, and I get in the hammock.

She talks to him coyly, tilting her head as she laughs at his stories. I feel plain and uninteresting. I feel ignored, and jealousy wells up. *Oh, brother,* I think. This is like summer camp. Sanctimoniously, I remind myself why I am here; to heal. Not to pick up men.

Sandy tells Puma of the headaches she has been experiencing. Not too long before we left New Mexico this last time, she had a car accident and hit her head on the steering wheel. She couldn't tell if the headaches were from the accident or detoxing from coffee, sugar, and salt. Puma offers to help her. But he first needed to go to his room to get his *Agua de Florida*.

A short time later he returns with a plastic bottle of yellow liquid. I let them know I'll be in the outside hammock resting.

A while later Puma finds me in under the palapa in the hammock.

"I finished with Sandy. She is resting. Her headaches will be gone now. Blood came out of her forehead. She's in bad shape. I could see a tumor," he says gravely.

How can he see a tumor? I wonder. I feel worried for her but decide not to tell her until she is feeling better about what Puma saw. I didn't want to plant the idea in her head. She might use it as a reason to die by making it real. Sandy did tell me before sometimes she gets such bad migraines – like when she eats too much chocolate or smokes too much pot – that she feels like she wants to die or might be on the verge of death itself.

With a twinge of guilt, my insecurities are petty compared to having a tumor in the head. I guess she can be the center of attention if she wants to be. I will flutter around the periphery as I always do. Resentment builds inside. I feel inconsequential in the whole scheme of things. But how will I change that?

I must have been thinking about that for a while. Puma sensed I wasn't interested in carrying on a conversation.

"Chao," he says, walking off with the bottle of *Agua de Florida* in his hand.

We get dinner tonight since there is no ceremony.

I go and see if Sandy is awake. I rouse her, and she tells me she is feeling better. Fortunately, her headache has disappeared.

Curious, I ask her, "What he did to make you feel better?"

She proceeds to tell me. "Puma told me to remove all my clothes, which I thought was a little weird, and step into the bathroom. He placed a hand on my head while reciting prayers asking for God's help. Suddenly, I turned white and collapsed on the floor. I felt so terrible." She gave me an anguished look and continued. "He kept reciting prayers, and then he took a mouthful of *Agua de Florida* and placed his mouth on my forehead. In a loud slurping motion, he sucked at my forehead. Then, you won't believe this part, he leaned over the toilet bowl, and he spat a blackish-red clot into the basin. Gross! He wiped his lips with the back of his hand. I could see my blood on it. Then he repeated that several times until he spat clear." She took a breath, "I started to feel better, and he helped me back to my bed. And then he left."

"Really? You had blood come out of your head? Wow!" I said with a little awe my voice.

"Are you ready for dinner?"

I wait for her to get herself together and we walk over to the dining room. Dinner is the usual simple fare, vegetables and rice. But of course, Marcos reminds us to eat as much as we can. We are losing weight. I don't mind. I'm towing around a few extra pounds.

In the dining hall.

Flat-out tired!

chapter forty

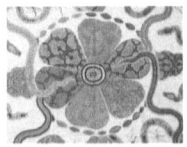

Ceremonies often start the same.

At first, I think nothing is happening, and usually, I am so tired I want to fall asleep.

The tired feeling is an inner resistance to what is about to happen and the nervous system adjusting. Other people also feel the effects of the medicine. There is a lot of sighing, groaning, and people trying to make their bodies comfortable.

I feel this miniature neon lime-green gargoyle creep up onto the back of my head and sit there. I keep telling it to go away, but I am distracted by all the visions. The black background with a variety of robotic insects move around all over the inside of my head and body. I'm terribly uncomfortable, and I start rocking back and forth like a crazy person.

I purge a little bit. The smell of rotting flesh exits my body, taking the *malos espíritos*, bad energy, with it. The robotic insects are back, like a wild rash they irritate me to no end. I can see them chipping away at the encasement that holds my fears.

The prison that is my life.

I keep saying to myself, I am never doing ayahuasca again!

Puma breaks my affirmation and leaps to his feet.

"*Dios Bendiga, yo soy lo más fuerte!* I am the most powerful!" he shouts along with a chain of other swears and threats.

I bolt upright, trying to pull myself out of the *mareación* I'm submerged in. I'm aware of the rise of tension in the room and the smell of gasoline. Marcos throws his lit *mapacho* sizzling into the basin and jumps to his feet and joins Puma. Both stand in front of me, spitting out the screened window right above my head. The spray lands in a fine mist and the smell of gasoline settles on my head. Worried my hair will catch fire, I reach for my blanket to cover my head.

"What is going on?" I interrupt Puma, hoping he'd explain the chaos.

"These devils, these *brujos* have arrived from the village. They want to fight me." He says before taking another mouthful of gasoline.

I keep thinking my blanket would smell. But when someone across the room lights a cigarette, I worry the whole place might blow up. To do my part, I call in Archangel Michael and all the other angels I can think of to help us.

The spitting eventually stops.

"Yah, they've left," Puma announces the departure of the *brujos*. He crumples to the floor, scratching around for his cigarettes. A flickering orange flame lights the end and a faint red glow moves through the blackness.

He sits smoking for a long time. He didn't stand up to sing icaros after that. He just watched the end of his cigarette burning as the ash fell off and landed in his basin.

The disruption left staleness in the air, and my body felt very heavy.

I couldn't wait for midnight when the ceremony would officially be over.

chapter forty-one

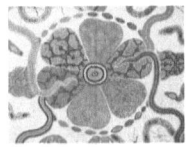

We take our usual seats in the ceremony hut. Puma places his *accoutrements* in their rightful places.

He tips the contents in the old plastic water bottle back and forth like an hourglass before he slowly opens the lid. No hiss of gas escaping this time. He brings the opening to his lips and whistles in his songs. He pours each of us our portion into the coconut cup.

Tonight, I decide to hold my nose as I gulp the foul liquid down my throat. It tastes bad still but slightly less, because my olfactory senses are dulled. I am very unceremonious compared to Giovanni. He takes the cup like he is accepting a gift of gold from the holiest of teachers. This, indeed, must be medicine because of how bad it tastes. I rinse out my mouth and wipe my lips of the residue, using the toilet paper sitting on the wooden floor.

A short while later, Puma blows the flame of the lantern out and lights another cigarette. I shut my eyes and try to relax against the hard wall. Faint lines begin moving against the black background. I feel sweat running down my spine. *It's so hot in here!* I push away the fleece blanket draped over my shoulders.

My head feels like it is detaching from my body and swimming far out in space.

Neon colors begin to appear, swirling and dancing on lines of electricity. I want these visions to stop. It is too much for me. I call out for Puma, "*Canta*, sing!" I hope the magic songs would distract me or transport me to anywhere but here.

I hear his Bible scratch the floor as he picks it up.

He then begins to recite his prayers. This seems to go on forever. Then with a final "*Dios Bendiga*" his voice leads into melodious icaros. They are in a language I don't understand. I catch a few Spanish words, but I don't care what he says. As fast as I got hot, now I am freezing. Wrapping myself up in my blanket, I sit and shiver uncontrollably. My legs are shaking so much, the backside of my knees knock against the floor. They seem to have a life of their own, possessed and jumping around in spasm. My mind is going crazy with all the neon geometric shapes shifting and transforming continuously.

I am totally out of control.

I see a giant serpent slither up the entrance steps and across the floor. The serpent dances the slow wine to the sound of Puma's voice. I open my eyes to see if there really is a snake in the room, but when I do, my eyes hurt, and I see only pitch black.

Closing my eyes again, I am afraid I will lose myself inside frenetic electric lines. I resist, bringing myself back into my body. I feel my legs thumping against the floor. I reach beside me to feel some human warmth and draw myself closer to Sandy's side. She gently puts her hand on my back and rubs in small circles.

"Breathe," she says softly. "Just breathe."

I inhale the humid air deep into my lungs. I exhale slowly, trying to bring my attention to my breath rather than what is happening to my mind. A couple breathing cycles later, I feel less afraid but my legs still jump like grasshoppers in a frying pan.

Across the room, Humberto tells me to control myself and be strong. I will my legs to behave and be quiet. They obey for a moment until my mind drifts again.

Humberto tells me more loudly, "You must make your body obey your mind!"

How?

I focus on stilling my wild legs again when Puma glides through the darkness toward me. He gropes into the blackness until he finds my head. With one hand resting on the top of my head, I hear him drink something. He brings his mouth close to my crown. With slurping sounds, he sucks something invisible from out of my head and spits into the bucket. Then between his two hands, he squeezes the sides of my head and then the front and the back. He releases his hands off my skull as he steps slightly away from me. He takes more liquid into his mouth and spits a fine spray of the spicy-floral *Agua de Florida* all over my face. With another mouthful, he spits down the front side of my torso. He steps closer and presses with a firm squeeze my chest and upper back. Satisfied, he says his usual, "Yah."

"Yes, *muchas gracias*," I respond, noticing that I feel pretty good right now.

He moves away from me and switches to a sharper icaro. "*Limpia limpia cuerpocito, de de de de de.*" Repeating the melody over and over he sings to the ayahuasca to act as a doctor to clean and heal us.

Then, the swirling starts again. I sweat profusely, drenching my clothes. I feel afraid to be alone, and I reach out to touch Sandy's leg, making sure she is still there. She reaches back. From beside me, I hear Giovanni rustling around on the floor. The scrape of the plastic bucket against the wooden boards and then the horrible retching sound as he purges his guts out. I shiver and send over a feeling of compassion to help make it seem less terrible.

Like a contagion, I feel the urge also. I sit up quickly, groping in the dark for my bucket. Just in time, as a freight train of heavy energy rolls out of my stomach into the bucket.

Inside the bucket, the redolence of rotting cockroaches wafts up around the perimeter of the bucket. I see yellow-lime shapes wriggle around in the soup before they vanish into the humid night air.

My head droops over the bucket, resting.

I am so tired. All my strength seems to have disappeared when more images of yellow-green demon creatures appear and the iron-horse rolls through me again, forcing even more violently another purge. Then another and another. *How much more?* I wonder.

I hear a voice, *"You're not done yet."* Instinctively, I massage my thighs, squeezing every square inch of volcanic rage out of my legs.

The fiery breath inside takes me deep into the core of the earth. I am here, lying in a yellow layer inside of the earth. I feel an unexplainable and overwhelming sadness well up and seep from my pores. Visions of a beautiful, dark-haired woman appear. She blows through me like the wind whispering through the aspens on a fall afternoon. She tells me something, not through her words but through the way she moves, and I know exactly what she is feeling. She shows me that I am embedded in a layer of uranium. When it is disturbed and removed from her belly by the hands of man, she is scarred and her entire life becomes endangered. In the vision, I see a charred and dying earth, blackened and desolate.

Her tears rain on the vision, and I feel her despair.

Suddenly, from the deepest recesses of my being, a dangerous hatred bubbles up like boiling tar.

I hate men.

ALL men.

All the men who had leered at me through my life. All the men who groped me growing up. All the men who had betrayed me, lied to me, and deceived me. I hate all the men who I let use me. I hate all the men who were weak and despicable. I hate all the men who thought they were more powerful just because they were born with a penis. I hate all the men who thought they could pillage and plunder and get away with their atrocities. I want to rage and tear them all apart, limb by limb and hang their genitals on a tree branch for the vultures to pick at slowly until their entire manhood is devoured.

I don't know what to do with myself in such a state of rage and hostility, and then I begin to cry. The internal violence transforms itself into a profound sadness, then grief. I grieve for my lost self. The parts that I have given away to men because I thought I should – and ended up as a wisp of my true self.

I realize I am the one who betrayed, lied, and deceived myself into believing that I wasn't worth hanging on to.

So, I gave myself away like a two-bit whore.

I'm as hollow as a dead tree eaten out by termites.

chapter forty-two

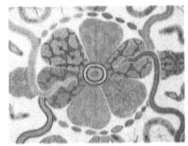

Hunched over crying, I sit wallowing in the wake of my self-annihilation. Self-pity overtakes me, and I step into death's downward spiral.

I am worthless.
I am nothing.
I am dead.
I lie back on the floor and let myself die.

My head is propped against the wall's wooden planks, my body paralyzed. My limbs are a mass of useless flesh strewn out before me. I look around the room. The maloca no longer exists. We are in a sultry swamp, somewhere in the middle of the Amazon. Across the room, the others look like newts and toads. Juanita sits next to me, fanning me with her translucent dragonfly wings. *It's so hot in this swamp. What the hell am I doing in a swamp?* I wonder.

I look down at my legs, which seem to be joined by the inside seam of my former thighs. After some concentrated effort and careful examination, I realize I am a tadpole in the very early stages of my development, for I can't yet swim. I can't do anything but lie here and sweat in the fetid humidity. In my mind, I ask, *"Why am I a tadpole in this swamp?"*

A voice answers me, *"You need to rest. You have just died, and eventually, you will be reborn."*

It feels like hours have passed.

Eventually, I turn into thick-skinned, grotesquely fat and ugly toad that burps and flicks its tongue out, catching mosquitos as they zip by. Through my evolution as a swamp creature, my body finally regains a human form.

But then, an intense burning and chewing sound echoes in the center of my head, a sound so loud I want to scream. I can't escape because it is inside me. I start to breathe, hoping to slow down my panic. I see millions of ants inside my head, eating my mind. Their chewing is driving me insane. *"Why are you eating my brain?"* I shout at them. The ant with the longest and slimmest body, the queen I suppose, steps into view. From her managing post she explains, *they must clean out all the obsolete garbage in your mind, and it will only take a few minutes longer.* Once I realized they are actually doing me a favor, I focus on my breathing and let them do their work. Their task complete, the queen ant returns, telling me that my mind has been reassembled in accordance with the vibration of Truth.

For several moments, I'm in complete and utter silence, dark and viscous like molasses. As if I am floating through the deepest, endless void at the galactic core. A silence where nothing is happening yet from which everything comes.

Then, out of nowhere the ferocious sound of a buzzing swarm of bees approaches. The volume increases the closer they get and fills up the empty amphitheater of my skull. The noise is so loud, it is all I can focus on. Bees buzz incessantly, keeping the vibration of their wings at top speed. Finally, I can't take it anymore, and I interrupt them.

"What is the Truth?" I shout out to anyone who would answer me.

A bee with a tiny golden crown appears before me with a regal air, *"I am Melissa, Queen of all the bees. We are re-*

calibrating your vibration to that of Infinite Love. You seem to have forgotten." She says with disdain, *"We won't be but a moment longer."*

I focus on my breath. Inhale, one, two, three, four. Hold one, two, three, four. Exhale one, two, three, four. Hold one, two, three, four. And again, until the sound of bees instantaneously ceases, and I am back on the maloca floor.

Puma winds down his magic songs and finishes with *"Dios Bendiga,"* our closing blessing of the ceremony. He sits down where he began the night, against the far end of the maloca and ignites the kerosene lantern. Lying flat on the floor, his head propped against the wall boards, he lights a cigarette and lets out a small chuckle. Infectious, we all laugh hysterically, like we have been at comedy central and not in the pits of Hell.

He reaches for his flashlight, illuminating his bulky metal watch, "It's very late. I am going to my hut," he says. The cue: it's time for us to leave, too.

I try to get up, but my legs are so tired and rubbery I can only lift myself onto all fours. As I crawl to the doorway, Humberto and Puma raise me to my feet and walk me over to the wall. I lean on the wall as Puma hands me my shoes. I shove my feet in and try to make my way down the steps but grasp the door jamb for support. Humberto swings my limp arm around his neck and walks me back to our hut, delivering me carefully to my bed.

A rag doll, I flop down as they unfurl the gossamer of mosquito netting above my head.

I mutter, "thank you," closing my eyes to the brightness of the candle flame burning on the shrine.

chapter forty-three

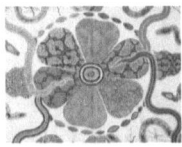

The following night, I take my usual spot sandwiched between Giovanni and Sandy.

I arrange my lumpy pillow behind me, propping it against the hard, wooden planks.

The flicker of the small tin kerosene lantern cast shadows against the wall boards, dancing to life the smoke curling out of the tip of Puma's cigarette. He lies on a blanket, ankles crossed with his neck crooked against the wall, pensively looking through space. His left hand rests reassuringly on the Bible's worn black-leather cover.

He flicks the stub of his cigarette into the plastic bucket near his feet. It sizzles as the last bit of life leaves it.

He reaches for the used Inca Cola bottle, now filled with a thick dark brew. He tips it back and forth a couple times. He twists off the yellow cap; a rush of air escapes. Setting it next to his bucket, he brings the rim up to settle under the curve of his bottom lip. Almond eyes closed, he whistles into the bottle. A shiver rattles through my body. And I try not to think about the taste of the drink I am about to consume.

He takes a half coconut shell from off the floor and pours the brew into it, measuring out a stiff dose for Marcos. Marcos walks over on his knees, taking the cup in both hands. He holds it like a prayer before tossing back the contents.

Sandy's back is to me. Her mesquite honey blonde hair ripples when she tips back her head. "Ughhh," escapes her. Then, *"Gracias,"* before turning around. She passes by me with a forced smile that lies, "It wasn't so bad," before taking her place next to me. She finds her water-bottle, takes a swig, swishes, and spits into the plastic tub. She quickly lights up a mapacho, sucking smoke into her mouth, her face starts to relax.

Now, it's my turn.

I scoot up to the edge of the blanket and kneel. Puma pours my dose. I take the small cup, hold my nose, and throw the bitter viscous liquid down the back of my throat, shuddering, *"Gracias."* I go back to my place against the wall. Sandy gives me another smile for reassurance and passes me a freshly lit mapacho. I inhale ferociously until the ayahuasca becomes a lingering memory.

I close my eyes and wait.

The liquid churns in my belly as the medicine starts to take hold.

An iceberg moves out from my core and melts on my skin. My teeth chatter. I grope for my fleece blanket and droop it over my head and shoulders.

The orange glow in the room blackens when Puma blows out the flame.

Darkness shrouds me. Only the neon colors emerging from my inner vision bring light. Like an old television set, it starts with a speck of white light before the full picture blooms upon the screen and a vision emerges. And, I am in the movie.

The sleek black panther brushes its luxurious pelt against my arms.

I melt into the velvety softness and the strength of his embrace. I lose myself in the grip of his bite on the nape of my neck. We tumble, teeth lost in fur. I am a cat. A large tawny lioness. Yet, I am human, too. I feel like a cat in my body. But I am myself in my mind.

He is playing with me. Feline to feline.

Back in the room, in my human form, I rock back and forth. Back and forth, I sit on the hard floorboards. Heat rising, I want to be ripped apart by those sharp and dangerous claws. Vibrations penetrate my body.

His beautiful voice sings the double helix serpents out of their hiding place deep within my womb. Wind and entwine and release and entwine, snaking their way up my spine. I keep rocking, back and forth, urging them higher, faster. I am sitting in the center of a fire, flames encapsulate me. The song infiltrates my blood. My cells come alive with desire.

I am going to ignite.

What is happening? What has taken me over?

The song!

Suddenly, I command my body to still itself. Fear creeps in and my skin prickles with goosebumps. I cool breeze whispers as it passes behind my neck. I jolt erect. Angrily, I become aware that something is happening that I can't explain. I encase myself inside an electric violet cocoon. The song's vibrations bounce off the force field, blocking the song's power, forcing Puma into another icaro. He moves to the other side of the room.

I realize I haven't been breathing. I inhale deeply, steadying myself. *What was that about?*

I'm losing control.

I must gain control.

chapter forty-four

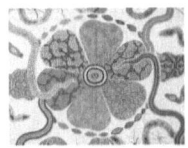

Silence feasts on the darkness, pregnant and ravenous with anticipation.

Puma searches blindly through the void.

Standing before me he pats my head, making downward strokes through my hair.

He touches a cheek gently, as a sign of recognition. I lean into his hand and let him cup my face.

This is strange. He's already done a healing on me. He's never done two on me before.

Clearing his throat, he waits a moment for the magic song to possess him. From his voice, a mixture of yearning and lament emerges as he sings a hauntingly hypnotic icaro.

My soul reaches out aching to be filled and entwines in its frequency. I sway slowly, undulating to this mesmerizing melody.

Suddenly, my body stiffens as the offensive odor of cheap perfume saturates my crown. Puma drags the smell across my face, trailing a path that lands on my chest. He moves a hair closer, pressing his hands on both the front and back side. Reaching into my heart, he leaves an imprint like memory foam.

He plants his palms firmly into my sacrum at the bottom of my spine, giving me one final press.

I'm curious about the source of this strange smell.

I open my eyes a sliver.

And, I see him twist a cap on a small plastic bottle that I've never seen him use before. He tucks it under his thumb, covering it with his right palm and slips it back into the front pocket of his pants.

Finished with my healing, he utters, "Yah." with a gruffness of someone who smokes too many unfiltered cigarettes.

"*Gracias,*" I respond, bowing slightly.

The black leather Bible in one hand and a maraca in the other, Puma amps up his icaros. The maloca quakes with the dancing rhythm. The energy climbs higher, seeking liberation through the cracks in the palm-frond roof.

About midnight, the ceremony complete, we walk Marcos and Puma across the little arched wooden bridge back to their huts in the swamp. Puma gives me a hug, a very affectionate hug. Not the usual stiff hug with a couple pats on the back, like the hugs people give each other who are afraid to feel close. No, this hug is intimate. As if a portal has opened between us.

Sandy and I retrace our steps on the dirt path, embraced by giant dark tree trunks and the cacophony of insects ushering us along.

Once back in our casita, I scoot the mosquito netting back and quickly fly onto my bed. Once inside I tuck the fabric under the mattress to keep any mosquitos from biting me. Then I lie down on the hard bed, taking a deep breath.

A flame flares beneath my sacrum, shooting liquid cayenne pepper up the channel inside my spine.

Ardent passion consumes me.

And, all I can think about his him. The shaman. Puma.

I can't sleep. I try. I take some homeopathic Calm. A little while later, I take a few droppers full of an herbal remedy. I put on my headphones to listen to some brainwave entrainment. But I am single-focused. Every thought is of Puma. Raging with fever, I strip down to my underwear and pile my clothes at the bottom corner of my bed.

Eventually, I relax enough to be in this Neverland place and doze off. But I am in a lucid dream state, neither awake nor asleep. Or both at the same time.

I look down at myself. My skin is now the pelt of a tawny lioness.

Puma transforms like liquid mercury from his feet up into a lithe black panther.

I pounce on him and chase him around, two kittens tumbling in the grass. I follow him to the lip of the shadowed jungle. He is toying with me, luring me to follow him. I feel no hesitation, only the pull; two magnets helplessly drawing together. I, a lioness, and he, the black puma.

I follow him into the shadows.

chapter forty-five

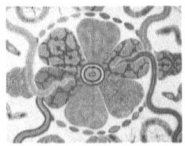

Puma taps the wooden screen door with a key, ratta tat tat.

His signature knock interrupts my thoughts.

The rushing river of my heart beats loud in my ears. Electricity races through my body and my hands shake. Quickly, I put on a tank top and capris before clawing away the mosquito netting ensnaring me.

"Hola," I say breathlessly, leaning on one foot as I push the door open.

He leaves his rubber boots on the bottom step, brushes past me and comes inside. The voltage between us creates an arc, joining us together with invisible wires.

We're standing face to face. I cross my arms across my solar plexus to keep myself from being pulled toward him. I do my best to keep a straight face and a firm lid on the continuously stoked fire raging in my loins.

He immediately starts talking without a "hola" back.

"Last night in the ceremony I saw you as a white angel of light." He pauses a second, then continues, "Did you know I'm an angel too?" he asks with the lilting quality of jungle Spanish.

I shake my head, no, and he continues, "And I put a crown of flowers on your head and that we were up in heaven, married."

I lean back onto my heels, giving myself space to think. And, more importantly, space from him.

"I was going to put a gold ring on your finger, but something told me to wait," he says slowly as if recalling details of the scene.

I remember now. He did put a gold ring on my finger, and I took it right off and gave it back to him.

It is coming back to me now. And that's when I smelled that stinky perfume.

The fight between what I know in my head to be true and my body's uncontrollable desire to be consumed by him ensues.

I stand there. Not sure what to do. Not knowing what to say. Feeling the fission of being split apart.

Raising his left eyebrow a couple of millimeters, he looks at me, waiting for a reaction or a response. I give neither.

Awkwardness infiltrates the room.

"Adios," he says, and rushes to the door, letting it slam. The wood steps creak on his way down, and I hear the soft padding of his rubber boots on grass as he walks away.

chapter forty-six

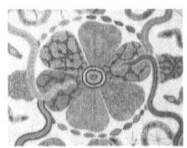

All I want to do is follow him around. To be next to him.

I seek him out.

He usually hangs out during the day under the palapa where they brew ayahuasca. Swinging, like a metronome, in the hammock strung with coarse sisal, scratchy and uncomfortable looking. He looks up, sees me approach. I put my hand on the hammock and follow the rhythm of its swing.

He seems cool, aloof. The opposite of his warm, affectionate self from last night. Confused, I keep feeling the swinging motion. Hoping he will say something. He does.

He talks about Pucallpa, where he used to live. And his plans for his life. How he wants to open a healing center. He continues talking about his vision and dream of a botanical center in Pucallpa. But, how he needs a partner to do what he wants.

"I see you and I working together," he says matter-of-factly. "You need to make a decision about doing this with me."

I'm confused. How did this conversation jump to a big decision like this? *Am I losing something in the translation?* I wonder.

Not once did he ask me my dream or desires. Nor, does he bring up the feelings between us.

He insists I make a decision!

"I don't have any *compromisos*, I have no commitments with anyone else," he tells me. "Do you?"

"I'm still married." I remind him.

Out of curiosity, I ask, "How many kids do you have?" Most Latin American men have a handful.

"I have three," he tells me. "I have a sixteen-year-old daughter from my marriage, another daughter who is eight and a four-year-old son, named after me." He continues, "The mother of my younger children cheated on me last fall. So I left. I wanted to get far away. That's why I came up here to Iquitos." He finishes, looking away.

His pain cramps my heart.

"What good is working if you don't have a woman?" He looks squarely into my eyes.

I shrug my shoulders.

The space between us feels heavy, like water weighing against me.

"I'm in no hurry to make up my mind," I remind him.

I unwrap my hand from its clutch around the hammock rope and begin to walk away.

He deftly rolls out of the hammock, landing on his feet. He takes a couple of steps toward me. I stop walking. Gingerly, he places his forearms on my shoulders. Holding me tight his solid athletic chest melds into mine. He attempts to kiss my lips. I quickly turn my face to the side, offering him a cheek instead.

He acts calm.

But the energy beneath his skin writhes like coiled snakes.

I fight to control myself. My only option is to break Puma's grip. And I push back, wrenching away. I force him to unclasp the hands that keep me locked in his possession.

He drops them to capture me around the waist. I pull back, just out of his reach. A furrow grows deep between his black brows. And, his eyes reflect the slash of rejection.

I pretend not to care.

Pivoting on my heel, I walk away. The volcano in me is about to erupt.

I don't want him to know how I feel.

I enter the casita and let the door slam.

"What is wrong with you!" Sandy asks. "You've been following Puma around like a lost puppy for days now! What is going on with you!"

I can't explain with words. I look into her eyes hoping they will transmit all the pain, frustration and confusion I feel.

"I don't know!" I say exasperated, dropping onto the bed with a thud. "I feel obsessed. I just want to be with him. I don't know why." I glance down at my hands, picking at a hangnail. "I'm so embarrassed! I never act like this with men. I feel so pathetic."

She gives me an "Oh, brother, you're ridiculous" look. Then she does a double take at me.

"Shhhhitt," she says, elongating the word. Shaking her head in dismay, she sits on her bed facing me, hands clasped between her knees.

I lean closer toward her. From the look on her face, this can't be good.

"I've heard about this," she says, more speaking to herself. "But I thought it was folklore."

"What! What is going on Sandy?"

"*Hechizeria*," she utters, a Spanish word I don't know.

"What does that mean?" I push her along to get to the point.

Behind pursed lips, she holds back what she's thinking. Then, looking me straight in the eyes, she says with finality, "I think Puma has put a spell on you."

My eyes widen in disbelief, "Huh?"

Waiting for more explanation, she continues,

"So..." she pauses like she has a lead weight attached to her belly, "so, you would fall in love with him."

I couldn't believe what Sandy said was even possible. I was a smart woman from a modern society where this sort of thing would cause laughter and be considered completely ridiculous.

I struggle, trying to rationalize the whole thing. But I can't rationalize away the feeling I have in my body.

I doubt if I could ever be free.

I had come all this way into the Amazon to get away from a controlling husband, and I end up in a worse situation. Too much of my life had been under the control of parents, school, society, and I didn't even know how to be sovereign. Perhaps the abandonment and abuse in my life have left me so helpless.

That there is no way out.

Maybe I was too powerless to control my destiny.

And, I have become my own slave master.

chapter forty-seven

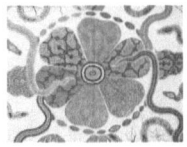

Shortly after breakfast, I head outside to rest in the hammock.

I lay there swinging; the stiff sisal rope creaking against the palapa's wooden post hypnotizes me. The little bird perched on a pole next to me chirps an alarm and flies across my belly.

The hairs on my arms stand up like a prickly pear.

The little bird gives warning that someone is coming.

I freeze. My senses scan the environment. The invisible danger transports me back in time to the house that wasn't even supposed to be a house. But a garage.

The miniature bedroom my sister and I shared had space enough for a bunk bed and a dresser. It was summer and hot. I had tricked my sister into sleeping on the top bunk while I slept in the cooler, cave-like lower bunk.

I must have been in bed asleep for hours when I felt a big, rough overworked hand reach up my tee-shirt. It scratched my belly before it landed on my small twelve-year-old breast. Paralyzed, my heart raced. I squeezed by eyes tighter, pretending to be asleep.

I held my breath.

I'd heard that if you play dead, a bear will leave you alone.

But this bear didn't.

A quick gulp of humid air brings me back to the hot afternoon jungle. My stomach clenched in fear. I realize I've been holding my breath. And, out of the corner of my eye, I see the empty hammock next to me begin swinging by itself.

Magically appearing out of nowhere, Puma stands at the foot of my hammock.

Weird.

Straddling space and time, my dredged-up past mingles with the present, leaving me feeling a little *loca*.

chapter forty-eight

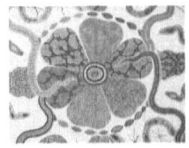

"Hey Marcos, would you mind if I popped by for a visit later?"

"Of course. Come anytime," he responds cheerfully.

"I might have a little nap first. I am starting to feel sleepy, then I will come by. Like in an hour or so?" I confirm as much as one can confirm on jungle time.

"Whenever you want. Just knock on the door."

Back at the hut, I lie down on the bed. Unable to nap, I dig out my journal from beneath my blanket. I scribble what I remember from the latest ceremony. And I record the bizarre happenings that I can't yet grasp, filing them away for later. This seems like an awful lot of effort, but I don't want to miss anything I am supposed to know. It is like taking notes at school. I thought I could study later and glean more important things from my experiences. I certainly didn't want to miss anything and have to repeat it in another ceremony.

I take the little wooden bridge, cross the narrow winding creek, and continue on the narrow sandy path past the bend in the creek where we had the mud bath. I continue walking; the trees hug the path, darkening the way ahead. Eventually, the path turns from soft sand into a boardwalk. In a clearing, I see four casitas lined up in a row.

I pass by the second hut, Puma's hut. I see the outline of his body and a cloud of grey smoke through the window screen. He must have heard me. Shouting hello, he waves, beckoning me into his hut.

"How are you today?" he asks, as if he's laced with amnesia from this morning's magic act.

I answer cautiously, "Tired. The ayahuasca kept me up all night."

"I slept about three hours," he says casually. "I do *mi trabajo*, my work on other clients, at night. I don't sleep that much. I usually get out of bed around five-thirty."

Impressed with his minimal sleep requirements, I ask him why he gets up so early. I don't want to appear like an idiot by asking him what kind of work he is doing in the wee hours of the morning. I assume it is some mysterious shaman thing.

Climbing into his hammock, "That is the custom in the jungle. It is cooler then. We go to sleep early since there is no electricity."

"Oh, of course." Disappointed with such a mundane response, I walk toward the door as Puma asks me, "How did you see me last night?"

What does he mean?

Not knowing how to answer, "Well, I was so busy vomiting and feeling uncomfortable that I really didn't pay attention. Thanks for helping me out. I really appreciate it," I tell him graciously.

The flesh on his cheek bones droops in disappointment. "You didn't see me as an Inca or a puma?" He waits a moment as I shake my head "no," going through my memory banks in case I might have missed something.

"I saw your spirit. It is that of a butterfly. A magnificent butterfly. You have a beautiful spirit," He pauses and then says with some gravity, "but it is not strong."

My instant reaction puts me involuntarily into anger. *I am, too, strong! He doesn't know me from Adam!* But then I ask, "What else did you see?"

"*Muchos diablos.* Lots of devils and *carga negativa,* negative energy."

Great! Feeling a sense of doom and hopelessness and not knowing what else to say, I push open the screen door, "Chao" and I let it slam behind me.

The boardwalk carries me above the swampy ground, and I make my way to the last hut.

Through a screen, Marcos shouts enthusiastically, "Hi, Georgina!!"

"Hey, Marcos," I shout back.

I step off the boardwalk, waiting on the steps for Marcos to open the door.

"Hurry, hurry!" he pants. "I don't want any more damn mosquitos in here. Get in here, sister, so I can close the door!" He scurries urgently behind me, slamming the door shut. He takes out a lighter and puts the flame next to the green mosquito coil that is the centerpiece of his room.

"Sit down." He ushers me to the narrow bed.

He notices me searching for an empty space to sit.

"Sorry. Let me make room for you." He shoves his books and pens up against the wall. A pen rolls between the crack, landing with a plastic crackle.

"Your bed looks like a rat's nest, just like mine does!" I tease.

"I don't want to have to get out of bed for anything once I'm in there for the night! What did Puma want? I saw you coming out from his hut!"

"He wanted to see how the ceremony went for me. Great if you like throwing up. You didn't throw up at all. How come?"

"Well, after a while you are more or less cleaned out, and you get used to the medicine, so you don't have to have your guts ripped out!" Marcos explains with patient authority.

"Apparently I have a lot of negative energy. That is what Puma told me. I didn't know I was that bad," I report, feeling dejected.

"Well, we are all carrying around a lot of shit. Don't worry. You will clean it up. You've got time." He smiles at me optimistically.

Switching the subject, "Would you mind doing a reading for me sometime?" Perhaps he could enlighten me on my *carga negativa* and the *hechizeria*. Marcos told me previously that he had been practicing tarot to pass the time out here in the swamp.

"Of course, I love to practice my reading skills."

"What do you do here all day and for all these months?" He has been here about three months. It seems like a rather long time to subject one's self to mosquitoes and fish soup.

He points to a tape recorder in his rat's nest. "I am trying to memorize icaros. I have them all taped and go over and over them. Puma's are very different from the other shaman that was here. He uses more Spanish words and not just Shipibo. I think he also uses Quechua. His teacher was Quechua from Cusco. But the other shaman, Victor, really didn't want to teach me anything. It was only during his last few weeks with me that he got serious about sharing. It was like he had resentment toward me. It was very frustrating. Then something happened with Victor and Humberto. I don't know what exactly but Victor was suddenly gone; 'poof.'"

He does an upward spiraling motion, rotating his hands like a flamenco dancer, "And then Puma showed up. The thing about that is I am supposed to have my own shaman and not be sharing with you guys. I like Puma, but he really isn't a "bush" shaman. He throws a lot of Christianity into his ceremonies. I came for an indigenous experience. Also, since I am on dieta and really I am not supposed to be associating with you guys, the *pasajeros*. My food is supposed to be brought to me. But because of the whole damned resentment thing I was telling you about, they would sometimes forget to bring me my food or bring it past the time I eat. One time I had to go to the kitchen and ask for my dinner! I got so fucking pissed off one day and told Humberto I wasn't paying any more money, so that might also be part of the reason why I am sharing." He gets off the edge of his bed where he had been sitting and locates his cigarettes on the window ledge.

Lighting up and swatting a renegade mosquito at the same time, "Bloody hell! They never stop do they?"

I laugh at his hostility toward the insects. "So, what other plants have you worked with?" I notice a bottle of something liquid next to his door and point to it.

"Oh, that is *To-eh*, the dreaming plant. I diet on it occasionally. It is supposed to give good visions and help find missing people or things that you have lost. Puma and I made it. He told me a story about how someone had broken into his house and stole some money and a gold chain he had. So, he drank some *To-eh* to find out who it was. Within a couple of days, he had visions of who it was: his brother-in-law! He also told me that to break out of *To-eh's* spell, you need to have a shaman do it or you could be trapped in the spell, forever!"

What if Puma had used *To-eh* on me? Would I be under his spell, forever? The thought stuck to me like a tick.

"Wow!" Hoping there is an easy solution, "How did he break out of the spell, then?"

"Since Puma has dieted on it, he has control over it so he can lift it when he wants to."

That isn't the answer I'm looking for.

I wondered about Marcos' reasons for taking *To-eh*. "So why do you diet on *To-eh*? I don't really understand the whole dieta thing."

"Well, you diet on different plants so their spirit will be a part of you. Once it is a part of you, it never leaves, and it will teach you about itself and what its purpose is. You can study all the plants from a textbook, but unless the spirit of the plant is within you, you will never know its teaching properties and experience its essence. For example, some plants like to work together, and some don't. Like ayahuasca and chacruna always go together, as a team; you can add others to the brew, too. Although I have only experienced a mix of ayahuasca, chacruna, and *coca*. *Coca* has great visionary properties, too. Victor made it for me once at the beginning. That made me see what was really going on around here."

He digresses. "Like they are all in it for the money and resent the gringos because they have money and feel like they are serving them. They try to take advantage. On the outside, they are smiling, but on the inside, they hate your guts. I think it is partly because Humberto is greedy and takes all the money for gambling and whores and the workers don't get paid, or they get paid late."

"That's disgusting! Isn't he married with kids?"

"Yes, he is, but that doesn't stop him. About a month ago, an Asian woman was here doing ayahuasca, and somehow, they hooked up. She thinks they are in love, but he is into her because she just got divorced and has a shitload of money. He thinks he will get it. For about a week, he didn't show up here at all because he was showing her around the country. Now she is gone, and there are new prospects. You be careful and tell Sandy, too. I've seen how she looks smitten with him."

"I'll tell her. But she might not listen since she saw them together in her visions."

I hear the door slam from the hut next door. Puma must be leaving for lunch.

"Marcos!! Lunchtime!" He bellows from the boardwalk.

"Looks like we'll have to have your tarot reading another time," Marcos says, slipping on his rubber boots. I didn't wear any shoes.

"Why do you wear your rubber boots in this heat?"

"Sometimes there are little brown snakes on the path, mostly later in the day but they are very poisonous and very difficult to see. You shouldn't be going barefoot. I almost stepped on one not too long ago."

I make a mental note to pay very close attention to where I put my feet and let Marcos break trail. Together we walk down the boardwalk through the swamp. There are two other little huts like those of Puma and Marcos.

"Are these for doing dieta, Marcos?"

"Yes, they are. Sometimes other people stay in them, too. I heard that next week a seventy-five-year-old woman is coming to do dieta! She will stay out here, too."

"That's crazy!" I am wondering why someone that age would subject themselves to this brand of torture. "She must be one tough old cookie!

Puma making medicine.

The casitas.

chapter forty-nine

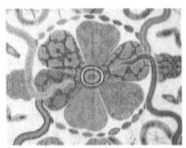

After lunch, Puma announces that this afternoon he will take us on a plant walk.

He will teach us about some of the plants and trees and their medicinal properties.

"Put on your anacondas," he reminds me. He's referring to my funky green and yellow spotted rubber boots. The workers say they look like an anaconda, especially if they have tipped on their side.

Puma's shout alerts us it is time for our walk. I slip barefoot into my rubber boots. Giovanni waits at the end of the bridge chatting with Puma. We cross the red stream, leading back down the path where the dieter's casitas are. At a fork in the road, we take a left, leading us back to the area where we had our mud bath.

Puma stops next to a huge tree and tilts his head way back, looking up. A large vine snakes its way around the giant. Near the bottom, a bulbous wooden growth protrudes from the vine like a snake's head.

"This tree is Grandmother of the jungle." We all tip our heads back, looking up and up in awe. Puma points to the serpentine-like head on a vine encircling the great tree, "And this is the spirit of ayahuasca, in the form of an anaconda."

He reverently caresses the tree, "It is a good idea for you to introduce yourselves to her and become friends with her. You can call for her help during the ceremonies."

We stand in the sacredness for a moment before continuing. We cross the clearing and step off the path into the dense verdant jungle. I'm thinking to myself, *it might be a long time before ayahuasca and I have a friendship!* Wielding his machete like a sword, Puma clears a small opening for us to follow behind him. After a short while, we stop. He reaches toward a thick loopy vine and grasps it with one hand, bringing it near us for closer inspection.

"This is ayahuasca," he tells us. I take out my camera and take a photo. I was expecting something a little more spectacular than a nondescript vine! I guess it is what is on the inside that counts, after all.

Still hacking his way through the foliage, we get to a tree with a blackish-gray nest attached to it. Puma calls this *"comején,"* which he says is a termite nest. It is for treating cancer and lung problems. He explains that it is cooked in honey. I'm amazed how so many things could be used as medicine.

We continue with our walk and Puma points out various trees and plants used for medicine. He explains that two spirits inhabit most plants and trees. One spirit has a beneficial side to its nature and the other has a malevolent side. We approach a large tree. Puma lays a hand on the tree and says, "This one, if you pin a photograph to it of someone you don't like, that person will die."

Giovanni and I look wide-eyed at each other. I shiver in disbelief. Continuing onward, we encounter plants that give you strength, many that cure cancer, and plants that can cure blood disorders such as diabetes.

Puma swings the machete into the roots of a palm tree he calls *chonta*. A white milky liquid escapes the wound.

"This one increases a man's libido. It looks like semen." He dips his finger into the viscous juice and licks it clean, smiling directly at me. Heat prickles the top of my ears, and

I quickly look at another tree. Giovanni and Marcos look at each other and follow Puma's example. Sandy and I start laughing at them as they hungrily lick the liquid Viagra from their fingers.

"What about for women?" I ask, feeling left out.

"Oh, we will have to cut some branches from *piripiri* and boil it up. It really is to strengthen the whole body. Men can drink it, too. If we come across some, we can cut some branches and get Juanita to help us cook it."

We do come across some plants that Puma selects for medicine. Laden with sticks, branches, and leaves, we walk in the general direction of the kitchen. He stops suddenly beside a forked-tree that looks like a pair of legs. He looks up at it and explains, "This type of tree is a *chuyachaki*. This tree inhabits the spirit of a *diablo*, goblin spirit. You could be walking through the jungle and come across someone in front of you who appears to be a relative or a friend. If you try to catch up and the person keeps walking like they want you to follow them, be careful! It could be a *chuyachaki*. It will take you far into the jungle, and you will get lost, and you will most likely never to return, and you will be turned into a *chuyachaki*."

"How do you know if it is a real person or this goblin?" Giovanni asks in amazement.

"Well, you have to look at the person's left foot. There will be something strange about it, and the person will walk with a limp if it is *chuyachaki*. Then you will know to ignore it, or turn around."

Giovanni's curiosity peaked, "How can you get turned into a *chuyachaki*?

"The spirit of the person gets stolen, and then their body is used to do things that the *brujo* doesn't want to be discovered doing himself," Puma explains.

As we kick through a layer of fallen leaves on the path, I wonder about what Puma just shared. A lot of bizarre things happen in the Amazon. This crazy stuff never happens at home. Or at least I have never heard of it. It is interesting how the spirit world and the material world mingle. In our culture, everything is so sterile and separate. Most people never consider anything that is not human, and sometimes animals, as having a spirit. And most people would never believe a tree could walk onto your path to trick you.

Back in the kitchen, Puma goes to work peeling the bark off the branches. Then, he carefully puts them in the pot on the two-burner propane stove. Next, he adds some leaves and covers it all with water. He instructs Juanita on how long to boil it for before departing to his hammock in the trees.

About four o'clock, Juanita rounds us up. She ladles a large scoop of the brewed medicine into our cups. "This is the last thing you can have before your ceremony tonight."

Chonta Palm

The bridge into the jungle, mud bath area and back casitas.

chapter fifty

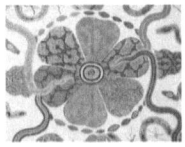

After much persuasion and guilt tripping from Sandy, Humberto decides to join us for ceremony.

She told him as leader of this center he should be joining us for ceremony and not hiding from what the medicine might show him.

He shows up, but he doesn't drink ayahuasca.

But, he did come to get a good *limpia*, cleansing, from Puma. "*Ven*, come." I hear Puma call across the darkness to Humberto in the far corner. A scuffle of a moving plastic basin and a small groan escapes Humberto as he gets to his feet and shuffles to the space in front of Puma. He kneels, and Puma pats Humberto's thick hair, marking his location. I look over at them as Puma amps up his cleaning icaro. Puma sings loudly. He jabs the melody like a knife as if to dislodge the energies sticking onto Humberto.

This draws my attention. I look up to see what is going on since I'm not heavy into the medicine anymore. Mounted on Humberto's entire back, a monitor lizard wraps its arms and legs around his arms and stomach. Inside the lizard is an orb-like creature with a skull full of razor-sharp teeth. I shiver looking at it. The way it cloaks him makes it seem as if the creature controls him. It's no longer Humberto but this thing that is using his body and stealing his energy.

My stomach feels queasy. I grope through my pile of mapachos that I have placed beside my blanket. I pick up one with shaky fingers and light it. I keep smoking and puffing and smoking some more. These aren't like regular cigarettes; they are super strong. I smoke one and a half mapachos and blow smoke on the creature. I use some color healing I learned when I used to do Pranic Healing, alternating pink and gold.

Sitting in the energy of this lizard creature and Humberto brings up thoughts for me around arrogance. This coincides with other demons barging into the maloca. I spend significant time pondering my own arrogance and narcissism. Psychologically speaking, I don't know what the definitions are, but those words came to me to label the experience I'm having. And, I didn't really know I was arrogant until right now. I don't even understand what that means. But I can see I have had ample opportunity to reflect on what that means in my life.

I feel left out when it seems Puma spends more time working with Giovanni, Gavin, and Sandy. He spends less time with me. And I'm usually last. It's a duel between not feeling important and feeling more deserving, and fluctuating between two sides of the same coin.

The ayahuasca teaches me more.

The coin of self-importance; one side arrogance and the other, narcissism, is a covering or protection against showing who I am to the world, which somehow leads to my purpose or what I'm supposed to be doing.

What am I supposed to be doing?

The words come as a voice, *"Your gift to the world is presenting yourself as you are. It's about being, not doing. And your talent is to be in integrity with that."*

And that's it? It seems too simple. How did I become convinced otherwise?

My body is flying, doing air acrobatics. I soar and dip and dive. I'm getting used to the feeling of liberty, freedom and being myself. Peace envelopes me, washing through each cell. I feel a tremendous amount of love for everyone in the room, for humanity, everything in the world. We are all one and connected. I can only be disconnected or separate when I think I need to defend myself. As if there is something so important about me that the importance needs defending.

My intention, for this ceremony, has been to experience Christ consciousness. Honestly, I don't even know what this means and a goal I picked up from the "spiritual" people I know. But I certainly got a taste of what it wasn't when my arrogance and narcissism kicked in. Well, hell, no wonder I'm not getting to the Christ consciousness part. I'm not vibrating at this level when I'm so worried about losing out or being superior; when I'm playing the victim. I need to learn to relax and receive instead of protecting myself inside a shield of arrogance.

I realize I have a lot to clear out – and gain a little, or rather, a lot of humility. I heard from the channel Lazaris that humility means "of the earth."

And that's *all* I want to do right now. To soak my head in that earthy colored creek outside the door. My brains feel on fire, and I have a throbbing headache from smoking too many mapachos.

I shouldn't be smoking so much. But, I really like it. I wouldn't usually allow myself to do this because it doesn't fit the image of who I think I am. *But who cares.* It goes against all the old rules of being good, being healthy, and trying to be perfect.

I play with the idea of smoking. I take the mapacho and put it to one side of my mouth or the other. I imagine myself as an old lady with rollers in her hair. Her cigarette hangs on only with a thin skin of saliva.

Free to Be You and Me– a song I used to love by Marlo Thomas – pops into my head.

If my purpose is to show up as me, that would seem pretty straightforward.

But I've forgotten what "me" is. I have so many layers of everything and everyone else on top of me. Through these ceremonies, I'm seeing how much shit I've allowed into my life. How much that isn't me, but I think it's me because I've been with it most of my life. Like my arm or hands, they've always been with me. I don't even know what the real me looks like. I just know that this isn't me. This scared and conforming woman isn't me, but shoes I've learned to wear.

When I was a kid, my step-mom laid out clothes she wanted us to wear to events she thought were important. I don't remember getting to choose my own clothes, probably because she knew I would pick jeans, a t-shirt, and no shoes if it were warm enough.

I can't remember at what age I stopped being me and the wild child was beaten out of me.

Above the stove, my step-mother had an oversized wooden spoon and rubber spatula. I can still remember the sound of wood scraping the wall as she removed one to smack me. As I got older, I ran around the antique, cherry-wood table in the center of the kitchen, and she would have to catch me first. Which she always did.

I got my last spanking at age sixteen.

My dad had a violent temper. I would see cats catapult across the barnyard with one of his swift kicks. We had three border collies to herd the cattle. Two were females, and one was a male. The two females refused to work for him because he yelled at them. They had their dignity, I guess.

One time my sister and I were quarreling, and he got up out of his chair, picked us up by the scruff of our necks like kittens, and smashed our heads together. I got a terrible headache, and I actually cried in front of them both. I always did my best to hide my pain from them so they wouldn't know how much they had hurt me. I didn't want to give them that satisfaction.

So, I can't really say when I stopped being me; after a while, it just didn't seem worth it.

The only problem is all that violence led me to be violent against myself. The first time I attempted suicide was at age fifteen. I didn't know what to do with the pain. My stepmother's solution was to keep moving. "Go outside and run around, you'll feel better." As I got older, that turned into running from all my intense feelings, especially in relationships. It was nothing for me to travel to the other side of the planet. In my thirties, I got tired of running and overworked myself instead. *I'll be fine if I just keep moving.* But I was moving further and further away from myself. As the years went on, it didn't take long before there was no one home.

In many ways, I relate to Humberto and that huge lizard riding his back. I have compassion for him, for me and for the wounded children in adult bodies who grew up in violence. And, who weren't allowed to be free. Most people believe this is normal, *This is life, and then you die.* Most people have no fire in their eyes, the light has flown away, and they seem dead; zombies going through the motions.

*****

After the skulls and the monitor lizard extraction from Humberto's back, Puma did one last epic spit into the plastic bowl.

"I have to rest for five minutes," he announces.

His ordinarily erect posture crumples.

He slides down the wall until he's lying flat on his back, ankles crossed and his neck crooked against the boards. He fumbles around to his right side, locating a cigarette, and an orange glow emerges. The peaceful darkness overwhelms the din of insect songs.

For some reason, the whole evening appears hysterical to me. I want to laugh my head off. I am looking at the game of illusion through detached eyes. And, some things are just ridiculous.

I look around the maloca, and I see perhaps I am the only one who thinks everything is a funny, gigantic, cosmic joke.

chapter fifty-one

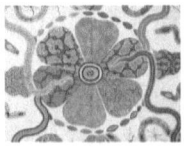

We lie a while not speaking, hoping the continuous cacophony of insect's singing would lull us to sleep.

"Can I blow out the candle? I want to go to sleep," Sandy asks.

"Could you leave it lit? For some reason, I am feeling afraid."

"There is nothing to be afraid of. I can't sleep with the light on, and we both need to sleep," she explains to me like I am a little child.

"Okay." Submitting to her wishes, I allow her to blow out the flame.

With the light exterminated, darkness comes to life.

Shadows and shapes sift past the veil of my mosquito net.

The scratchy scamper of rat's claws run across the rafters and descend the pole right behind my head. They land with a familiar thump and scuttle under my bed. I cover my head with my pillow, hoping to drown out the sound. Then, the ruckus seems to have moved into the attached bathroom. Extracting my head from beneath the pillow, I look around. I take a deep breath to slow my pulse, convincing myself to try to sleep.

But to no avail.

I lie there thinking about the ceremony. A lot happened, and I still don't understand what it all means. I will write in my journal tomorrow, maybe that will help. Sandy told me that a significant portion of the healing doesn't actually occur until weeks or months later. All I know is that it brought up a lot of feelings I didn't realize I had buried inside.

I call into the darkness, "Sandy, are you sleeping?"

"No, the rats are keeping me awake, and I'm not feeling tired. Why are you awake?"

"Well, the rats sound like they are having a party under my bed, and I am afraid of the dark. Did you know that when I was a kid that if my sister wouldn't wake up to go the bathroom with me, I would pee the bed? And when I go camping with Doug, and he won't go to the outhouse with me, I make my dog sit outside until I am finished. I have been afraid of the dark as long as I can remember."

"Why? There is nothing in the dark that you can't see in the daylight," she says, trying to assuage my fears.

"That isn't true. I see little things running around and shadows and shapes moving that I don't notice in the day. It is like my other senses are more attuned when my eyes don't see as well."

"That makes sense, but you are not a child anymore, and those things won't hurt you."

"Maybe." I get quiet, convincing myself that what she says is true.

It feels like hours have passed when this time, Sandy calls out across the void, "Are you sleeping?"

"No, of course not!" I laugh. "I am even not tired! Every cell in my body is vibrating. Electricity is surging through my veins. I feel totally amped up on speed or something!"

"Ayahuasca is a nighttime plant, so it is normal not to be able to sleep."

Well, I definitely agree with that. Sleeping at night as become a rarity.

To fill up the time, we continue talking.

Sandy begins by telling me about her trip across Africa and how she nearly died. She took an overland trip on one of those rugged truck-like buses. They drove down an extremely narrow road lined closely with trees. She decided to stick her head out the window and as she did, a tree almost ripped off her head. She missed it by millimeters.

Then she told me about the time she and several other people from her tour got so sick that the whole group was held up for a few days until they were strong enough to travel. They ended up staying in a small village by the roadside and sleeping in a shack on camping cots. Eventually, her fever broke, and she got out of bed. She was the first one out of the hut, and as she walked past the locals, they all clapped for her, chanting in Swahili, "Sister, sister," welcoming her back from death and her sojourn in the underworld.

Our many hours of talking finish when morning's peach glow peeks through the screened window.

I feel less scared with the emergence of the sunshine. The ayahuasca's effects have diminished in my body, and I decide to try for a nap before breakfast.

Sandy wakes me up a short while later with a cheery, "Breakfast time!"

Still sticky from all the sweating I did during the ceremony, I stumble to the shower. I gasp as the water chilled from the night rains down on me. I reach for the soap and notice the gouges and gnaw marks. Someone has been eating my soap! A trail of tiny, oblong poop gives the guilty party away. Damn rats! I gingerly pick it up and roll it around in my hand as I rinse off rat germs. Yuck!

Showing Sandy the teeth marks, "Can you believe the rats ate my soap?!"

She laughs. "I think we should borrow a cat from the kitchen for the night. Maybe that will help keep the rats away."

chapter fifty-two

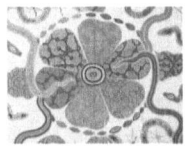

Someone shrieks from the opposite side of the maloca.
"Fuck!" In an English accent. "A rat just ran across my foot!" It's Gavin.

I laugh out loud as the rat scrambles its way through feet and legs and whatever else is in its way, to get to where it wants to go.

Not long ago, a rat jumped from the horizontal board on the maloca's walls and landed like a fur hat on my head. Then it vaulted into the center of the room. I screamed and frantically brushed the top of my head to get the weird feeling of its little rat claws off my scalp. We were all deep in the medicine. Everyone thought I was in a vision I believed was real and told me to calm down. Well, it was real!

After that, I became acutely aware of the rat's world. I could hear a rat calling to another rat in the maloca's bathroom. I could see a telephone-like cable made of light, maybe more like a fiber optic cable, strung between the two rats. I watched their squeal. A plasmic ball of light formed, following the line until it reached the second rat. Curious, I asked the rat what its purpose was and what they do. They'd tell me, the rats said, if I left a treat for them.

So, back in my casita, I put a rice cake in the corner of the bathroom where one had gnawed my soap. They ate the rice cake and kept their word.

Their purpose is to clean up all the human mental, emotional, physical, and psychic garbage. *"Humans not only put physical trash into the environment but their judgments, their resentment, their hate, their fear, their victim mentality and, in general, lack of self-responsibility. This pollutes all planes of existence unseen by your eyes."* The rat continues, *"That is why we appear so busy, running here and there because we have so much to do."*

I realize all the creatures of the jungle are here helping me, even the rats. They work very hard assisting me to remember who I am.

A wake-up call. I guess it literally took getting knocked on the head.

chapter fifty-three

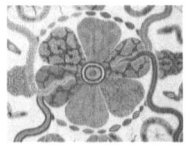

I can see death laughing at me from behind Sandy's pale, sunken eyes.

Her yellow skin stretched tight across her protruding facial bones. She appears a skeleton on the verge of death.

I try not to look at her. She's freaking me out.

She believes a lot of *brujeria*, witchcraft, has been put on her and that they are trying to kill her. I don't know who "they' is. But it seems like a collection of people she has met in her life. She is becoming paranoid and talking like a crazy person.

Marcos had told me a woman had died here while on dieta. I told him about the footsteps I had heard from my bed one night. I'm afraid and tell her I think we should leave. I'm worried about our safety. And if we will make it out of here alive.

To make matters even worse, they aren't feeding us properly. I would even welcome fish soup at this point. Juanita is doing her creative best to make the sparse food options stretch. She even sent Puma to the little store in Jan Chama to get noodles, rice, some plantain, and bananas. Humberto hasn't brought us any food from the city in a while. And I guess the workers haven't been paid in a while, either.

Sandy wants to get something to eat. So, we take the foot-path, muddy from the rain, to the village.

We enter the shack of a store that doubles as a restaurant. We pull a couple of stools up to the plank-counter and order chicken and rice. I get terrible stomach cramps that make me feel sick. It could have been from the Coca-Cola I had or something worse we picked up.

chapter fifty-four

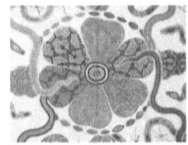

I seriously debate whether or not to leave the next day. Sandy's death mask, the games and brujeria, and the clincher; the lack of food.

But that night, surprisingly I fall into a slumber as soon as the mosquito net is secured and my head hits the pillow.

I don't know how long I've been asleep when a rat lands with a *boom*, right next to my head. It yanks me trembling out of the underworld, shaking me from a terrifying dream. At the exact moment, the rat startles me from the nightmare, I'm about to be raped.

Sweat pours from my body, soaking the black and ivory Shipibo textile that functions as a sheet.

Images of the dream flood my mind, drawing me back into the experience. I'm fighting to free myself, but I'm bound with rubber bungee cords, my legs forced apart in a wide "V."

A deformed caricature of Doug with an over-exaggerated penis protruding like a bent flagpole. A wild sneer contorts his face. The rat jumped a nanosecond before penetration, saving me from being psychically raped.

In the dream, gnarled knuckles hold down my head, and I am forced to perform fellatio. Doug's lolling wolf-like tongue drips with the stench of rotting flesh onto the back of my neck. I'm confused because he doesn't look like this at all. As if my thoughts and mind are no longer my own, I feel coerced and manipulated, doing whatever grotesque sex act was bidden of me.

I quake, it feels so alive and still crawling through my body. I feel like a whore. And watched by an invisible audience.

Some dark force has control of my dream. It is using Doug to fool me because he is my husband.

I'm terrified.

At the exact moment this is going on for me, Sandy is having a nightmare, too. The rats woke her up the very instant something awful was going to happen to her. She woke up swimming in sweat. Both of us are scared out of our wits; some evil forces are at work in the room and in our psyches.

Sandy even asks me to crawl into bed with her.

She never gets scared.

The rats go wild, running and thumping around on the beams and floor. I keep getting the shivers, like when a spirit passes you by, and you suddenly get cold. The mosquito net blows wildly as if a winter gale sweeps through the room.

I gather some courage. Crawling away from Sandy, I get the sage burning. I smudge the room and inside the mosquito netting, nearly smoking us out. I remove the Black Madonna card from the altar and read the prayer aloud,

"*O wise, miraculous Mother of Light*
With the mystery of Creation within you
Let your torch of wisdom burning bright, bring me safely through."

I repeat it several times until the rats have calmed. Then as quickly as they had become quiet, they go into another frenzy.

I scramble to get under the netting. Side by side, holding hands, we pray, "Our Father who Art in Heaven, hallowed be thy name…"

And then, I sing, "Angels we have heard on high…" even though I couldn't remember all the words. I call on Jesus and Mary and all the angels and archangels. Eventually, the rats quiet down, and the energy in the room seems peaceful.

Then it starts all over again, hurling the rats into a frenzy.

This goes on most of the night. I don't sleep at all.

In the morning, I glance over at the altar where I keep my piranha teeth. Usually, they rest on the miniature mountains of my citrine crystal placed in front of Ix Chel and the Black Madonna. They aren't in their place. I look down at my feet where they are smashed on the floor.

Goosebumps prickle the back of my neck. I'm seriously freaking out. And fear found its way back in.

Sandy thinks it was Puma punishing me for rejecting him.

He comes around early that morning.

Just after sunrise when the air still has a gentle glow I hear footsteps on the path leading up to our door.

They pause at the bottom of the steps, waiting.

I get off the edge of the bed and peek out the screen. It's Puma. He doesn't come any closer, but in a hoarse whisper, he calls Sandy's name. She's still asleep and doesn't wake. I feel irritated and suspicious.

Marcos had told me about this. The brujos come by and check their work. The lack of sleep and the disgusting nightmare left me raw with rage. I had had it with sexual abuse not just for me, but also for abusing the feminine. It is so prevalent at the center. There are a lot of sexual issues here. It's like a plague and everyone is infected.

At the breakfast table, Puma swoops by to say good morning. He leans with both hands against the end of the table, chatting with Marcos and Giovanni.

Casually he mentions that he took To-eh, the dreaming plant, last night.

chapter fifty-five

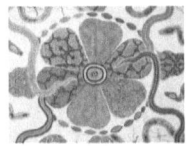

Making a beeline, I march across the open grassy area behind the casitas.

Humberto sits at the dining room table, eyeing me as I storm right for him.

Without removing my flip-flops, no "hola," no pleasantries. "I need to talk to you," I demand through the screen window.

His eyebrows crinkle in the middle, "Let's go outside."

He leads me to the picnic table located between my casita and Giovanni's. We sit face to face. He waits expectantly as I put together what I want to say in Spanish.

"Puma put a spell on me," I announce matter-of-factly. He raises his eyebrows, and his eyes widen with the word, *hechizeria*.

"That's not possible!"

"Well, it's true. I saw him put a little bottle of something in his pocket after he covered me with perfume."

"No." He's still not believing me.

"And, then I felt I was in love with him!" I'm frustrated because he's not believing me. Then I begin to doubt that my Spanish is getting across to him, what I'm really trying to convey.

I continue, "And, then, he attacked me in my dreams, too!" I glare at him, expecting him to say something to fix this.

But Humberto denies that none of this could happen here, at his center.

Furious, I want to escape his denial and my own helplessness.

I swivel my legs out from under the table and over the bench. "Chao," I say gruffly and stomp to my casita.

The casita groans as I plonk myself in the hammock. I kick the wall and begin swinging madly.

The hammock's rhythm soothes some of the anger.

Now, I'm more fed up of feeling powerless and afraid than I am pissed off.

chapter fifty-six

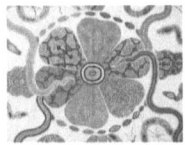

My grand intention for tonight's ceremony is to release all my fears and childhood traumas.

This seems a reasonable enough intention, considering what I've been experiencing here in Peru.

When a ceremony begins, I can never tell how it will go. Not much happens in the first half hour or so until, the ayahuasca kicks in.

And then it does.

For about three of the next four hours, I'm in absolute torment. I think death will come and claim me. I'm petrified of everything. I can't link my terror to anything in particular and nothing I can put a name to. The fear comes from somewhere far off in the galactic soup and swims up through my cells. Yawning heavy sighs and shudders, my nervous system releases. I have to keep moving my body. The pressure under my skin feels like some unnamed force would burst out through the thin epidermal barrier. My ears explode with the sound of insects. The whole Amazon jungle is consuming me, and it's driving me crazy.

I can't take it anymore. I need help.

Puma and Maria's mother, Inez are talking in Shipibo. They feel a mile away instead of just five feet in front of me. A wave of paranoia engulfs me. I'm sure they are conspiring and talking specifically about me. I want to break up their conversation and get rid of this overwhelming fear.

"Puma!" I call out.

He doesn't hear me.

I call a couple more times until he answers. He walks on his knees over to where I'm curled in a tight ball beneath my blanket. I sit up, and he pushes it back off my head. He takes a swig from the Agua de Florida bottle. With a gurgling sound, he places his mouth on my crown and sucks out the mareación, the intoxication along with some of the crazy. I begin to feel better and at a manageable level of paranoia.

He leaves me and begins singing in front of each person. He starts with Giovanni. I feel his icaro is meant to remind Giovanni of his shamanistic abilities. Next, he goes to Sandy. He sings a sharp staccato tune that is was meant to match her anger and fire and help mellow her out. When he gets to me, he sings a sweet, sad melody, making me cry.

Before that, I was feeling a poisonous cocktail of anger and jealousy.

I feel left out because he always picks me last. I'm struggling with self-worth, self-pity and not feeling special. I feel like the others are getting special treatment and I am left alone to wallow in my fear. I work on letting go. But I'm afraid to leave the prison of my perceptions.

Once, I do leave completely, and I convert into an eagle, and fly way up in the clouds. My body feels light and free, navigating through the sky. I feel my heart pounding, and I lose concentration and plummet back into my body. During one of the moments when I feel especially tormented with terror, a strong athletic woman appears, reminding me of my inner strength. She has a fierceness in her eyes and emanates a sweet tenderness. *"You know you're not special."* She says, causing a pang in my chest. *"Everyone has fear, but most bury it under the busyness of life. The trivia of life hides it deeply until you have a crisis, or until you die. Then you have to face this fear, which kept you from really living and going for your dreams and rising above the status quo. You thought you would die if you did. It is the fear of dying to survive, but the greater fear is the fear of not reaching your potential set out for you in this lifetime. Your fear is being seen and heard in your potential because it goes against the invisibility you created to protect yourself. Now we can safely say, that bridge has been crossed."*

She fades like fog from my vision. And stillness envelopes my body.

The insects' sounds ascend the space in the maloca, lifting and evaporating into their rightful place, outside in the jungle's night air.

Giovanni left for the airport this morning, leaving a gaping hole in our small group.

We don't have any ceremonies over the next three days.

I look forward to eating regular meals and resting. But the paranoia and fear has followed me beyond the maloca's walls.

I'm on edge; every little thing makes me jump. Hypervigilant and sensitive to everything, I think everyone is whispering about me and talking behind my back. I stay mostly buried under my blanket, hidden behind my veil of invisibility and the mosquito net.

Sandy checks in on me to see what I'm so scared of. I can't explain it, and I want to be left alone.

I have felt jumpy for as long as I could remember. Loud voices scare me. Loud thumps scare me. Doors opening and closing scare me. Silence scares me. Darkness terrifies me. Spiders terrify me. Rats scare me. What I feel from other people scares me. Things I know but can't speak about scare me. I'm so wound up in a tight knot, and I don't realize it until just now.

A few years back, I had gone for Eye Movement Desensitization and Reprocessing or EMDR for short. The therapist held her pointer-finger about nose distance in front of my face. She moved it left to right, back and forth, quickly and repeatedly. As my eyes followed her finger, images emerged and evaporated, releasing my internal pressure. But obviously there was a lot more still in there. My counselor said I had post-traumatic stress disorder. I thought that was only for Vietnam veterans and soldiers who had killed people and were shell-shocked.

I guess I am shell-shocked too.

And now I'm moving through being scared, and feeling all the scars and scabs.

chapter fifty-seven

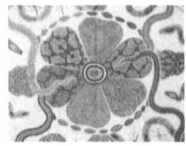

I feel as if I'm walking through thick, heavy clouds of tar. The energy is so dense in the maloca that no one feels the love at all.

Even Puma's singing sounds as if he's pushing the words out of his lips. My belly hurts and feels as if it has a bucket of vomit sitting on the bottom of it.

A black widow's sticky web, I can see all the clandestine entanglements between people in this room and of the center, too. I feel disturbed and disgusted.

Juanita told me, Don Juan, the head man here and Humberto's father, has an eleven-year-old girl-friend in Jan Chama. She said that sort of thing is normal here. The girl who took Sandy and Giovanni canoeing is thirteen. She moved here from Iquitos with her nineteen-year-old boyfriend. We saw her at a party we went to on Saturday night, and she was dancing, encircled by older men. Part of the reason they watched her was because her favorite move was to shimmy her chi chis, her boobs. I cringed watching her. The guys leered and laughed, which encouraged her to do it more.

It seems as if this whole place has a secret undercover sex life that is supposed to be hidden, but I can feel it. I guess I thought a healing center would be above this type of behavior. I thought everyone would have worked out their sexual issues and would be coming from a higher, more spiritual place. They are pretending everything is "normal," but it's not.

Maybe I'm supposed to see all this, feel all this and clear it from my system.

All those years of childhood I spent hiding, pretending I was invisible so I wouldn't get noticed. All those years being afraid. I finally realize how taxed my nervous system really is. I don't have energy left for me, my dreams.

Feeling lost, I'm floating on an ocean of sadness.

Icicles run through my blood.

With one huge heave, I purge the heavy bucket of rage that sits in the bottom of my belly. I feel lighter. It is as if someone has opened the door and let a warm breeze flow through the room. I start a teeth-rattling shiver. I'm beginning to thaw and release the sexual abuse from my system.

Intense pain shoots through my spine and travels out through my limbs.

It reminded me of helping my dad during a blizzard. We put boards over the barn windows to keep the heat in for the cows and their calves. I wasn't wearing mittens because I couldn't hold the nails to hammer them in. I didn't know how badly I had frozen my fingers and hands until I was back inside the warm house. I cried in agony as my flesh warmed up. There was nothing I could do but endure the process.

I really don't know how long this went on. Time has a mind of its own during a ceremony. My body relaxes the warmer it becomes. It is as though my body can breathe again. A flood of energy rushes through me, injecting me with a surge of vitality.

I begin to feel hope, that maybe, I'm not so broken after all.

In my visions, Jesus appears. I hesitate, considering my anger and rejection of him from my church-going days. But he puts his hand gently on my crown. The closed, creaky doors of my heart open. The energy flushes down my arms until my palms feel like hot burning suns. I can't contain the heat, and I hold them out, showering golden light throughout the room.

The impulse strikes me to call whatever I want into the room. And so, I do. With a thought, like magic, Mary with her guiding light appears. The angels, people I know, animals, places I want to go. I realize I have the power to have everything I imagine. I just need to ask for it, desire it and be joyful and grateful.

As the ceremony draws to a close, I feel no more rage, no more anger.

My body feels soft and supple and springy like Jell-O.

chapter fifty-eight

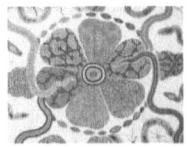

Throughout the next day, I contemplate power and my relationship to it, or should I say, my lack of relationship to it.

I realize I don't know much about power and find the whole thing confusing.

I'd either given it away or had it stolen.

I feel, weak, overcome and constantly compromising myself.

I'm guessing power must be the opposite. From the looks of it, no one around here has power. Even the brujo attack. What are those brujos doing? Nothing but tricks to scare someone else. If you can get someone to be afraid, you can control them. That doesn't seem to be power, just manipulation.

Even Puma with his spell. He overtook my will and brought up such a fire in my belly all I could see was lust for him. And I think it's love. I'm mesmerized by what he has done to me, exciting a part of me I'm terrified of. He put me up against my own fear, my fear of being a sexual person. My fear of showing off my femininity, my fear of being a woman.

I've been hypnotized into believing woman are good only for certain things; mostly as breeders and servants. I have never learned to value myself as a woman. Here, I've seen all kinds of things where women are degraded and used. Those young girls in Jan Chama don't know any better. They think they are somehow special, trading in their innocence for much older men to use their bodies for their own satisfaction.

I kept that part of me in the dark. Ashamed of what it could do and that it was wicked and foul and I should be modest and cover myself up. I should fit the norm of a good, obedient woman. Never complain, always comply. When the light of the spell shone on me, it woke me up, the energy within me. The silent sleeping power has come to its senses, and here I am now, contemplating my destiny.

This acceptable control over indigenous people, women and kids; those who are physically weaker – that seems to mean power. All those priests and governmental people who on the outside look so proper and together. But, in secrecy, they traffic humans and molest kids, and do ritual abuse. Does everyone think this is permissible? Or do they just not care or are too afraid of their own survival to say anything about it? No one seems to have power. They all give it away to someone who acts stronger. And up the chain, it goes.

I wonder when and where it will stop?

The only way it will stop is for those victims, the ones in fear, the ones who gave up their power, to gather their courage and use their voices and share what's going on.

When my sister and I decided to confront our father about our sexual abuse, he never apologized. He never said his behavior was wrong. He turned it around and tried to convince us he was our savior; he had convinced our mother not to abort us. So we were lucky to be alive. Somehow, this evened the score.

We didn't get the remorse we were hoping for. We didn't get the big family make-up we wanted and be able to go forward in our lives filled with love. I felt the brunt of the guilt for calling him out and disrupting his illusion that we were a happy family.

Remaining silent makes the violence seem okay.

I walk around with that guilt as if it is my fault I was sexually abused. People tell me that it is karma, that in another life I probably abused him. Maybe so. But in this life, I have to heal and repair the damage it has caused so I can move on and live what I came here to do.

During the psychic attack, I used my voice to chase away the darkness and violence. I sang songs of love, and called in angels and beings who knew love and compassion. That is the only thing that stopped it. And the rats were a big help, consuming the psychic garbage that spewed out into the night.

I am beginning to believe that the grotesque dream I had before coming to Peru foreshadowed what I would experience here to give me insight into humanity's sexual debasement in general.

I've asked Puma several times, but he still denies putting a spell on me.

And worse, I can't help myself, the way I yearn for him.

chapter fifty-nine

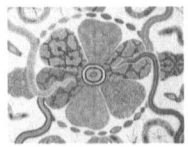

At twilight, I go into the dining hall.

My mission: locate one of the orange cats that usually sleeps outside in the woodpile behind the kitchen.

My eyes adjust to the darkness.

I can barely see, and I nearly tread on a mess of long black hair strewn like a fishing net about the floor. Tucked next to the counter, the saucer-sized eyes of the surprised woman peer over the shoulder of the short, dark-haired man lying on top of her. She quickly adjusts her skirt and sits up. Reminding myself why I'm there in the first place, I look away and keep moving to the woodpile.

I'm in luck, there is still a cat hanging out. I scoop him up, turn around and walk right past the two of them still in a heap on the floor. I have definitely interrupted something clandestine.

After breakfast the following day, I take my dishes back to Juanita. She leans close, whispering in my ear and laughing hysterically at the same time. Sputtering, she tells me I walked in on Inez, don Juan's wife and the handsome worker with the amazing smile, who is probably less than half her age. And they are having an affair! No kidding. No one is immune, it seems. This place is like a soap opera. Always some drama going on!

I don't know if it's the hot and humid jungle and lazy afternoons in combination with the ayahuasca. But I've come to the conclusion that this alchemical combination inflames the sex chakra. When the sex chakra is activated, of course, people feel horny and want to have sex.

Everyone here is on fire. Everyone seems to have that chakra activated. Then the only thing they know what to do with such powerful energy is have sex.

What about moving the energy to be another expression? Instead of creating a new life form, as in reproducing a child, put it into something creative. I wonder about this. I haven't been exposed to this type of possession on epidemic proportions like I have here. I notice it everywhere.

I feel it in me, too.

I'm judging others, even though I had an affair. I let my yearning take me down the rabbit hole. Maybe I'm here to observe how it works and make a better choice for myself.

It seems to me that what the medicine teaches is that there is always a choice.

Utilize the freed energy by having sex to dispel the pressure or channel it into something more honoring and creative. When Puma used the love potion, I felt the kundalini rise. I felt my heart open as the energy moved from my sex chakra and shot into my heart. By the time it hit my crown, I felt love for the whole universe. I don't understand it all except I feel so much love and that, in itself, could be addictive.

I could translate that feeling as the urge to have sex.

But I'm not going to.

We're supposed to be on dieta and abstaining.

chapter sixty

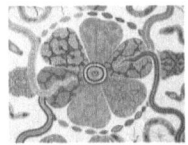

Sandy gives Humberto an ultimatum.
If they are to have any sort of friendship, he needs to drink ayahuasca with her.

So, he and Emilio, his cousin who behaves like his personal servant, join the ceremony. Puma calls Humberto up to where he sits at the end of the maloca. He gives him a *limpia*, cleansing and arcana, a protection song. A short while later, the ayahuasca must have kicked in, and Humberto starts blabbing to Emilio in Shipibo, and not quietly either. Then he begins belting out his own icaros.

I lean toward Sandy, "I wish he'd stop singing! He sounds like he's singing Irish lament songs!"

"Aren't they beautiful?" she says, glancing at him with admiration. "He learned those from his grandfather."

Yuck! I roll my eyes.

He completely drowns out Puma's icaros, and I have a difficult time singing along. Then Humberto turns into the shaman. He decides he needs to give us all fire *arcanas* for protection for when we get home. He clumsily gets up on all fours and staggers to his feet. He shuffles over to each person, still belting out his icaros.

This whole time I'm angry and resentful that he's commandeered the ceremony. Moreover, I'm pissed at Puma for not having the balls to tell him to shut the hell up and sit down. My brain is getting confused and annoyed with the racket. I keep trying to focus on one thing at a time; either Puma's icaros or Jesus' hand on my head.

Humberto eventually gets to me.

I'm full of resistance. I put my blue pashmina scarf over my head. Humberto instructs me to hold my palms open, face up, in receiving mode. I do for about ten seconds then cross my arms over my solar plexus to shut down my energy field. He leans forward and tells me the arcana isn't working. Of course, it isn't! And he pushes the scarf off my head and blows smoke on my crown.

Now, I've got a bad headache.

Following the ceremony, I'm super annoyed and angry. To make things worse, Sandy invites both Humberto and Emilio to sleep in our room for the night, before she asks me if it's all right. I don't want to make waves, but I'm not really happy about it, considering how I feel about their negative energy.

Humberto selects the hammock and Emilio sleeps on the floor like the family pet. I really can't stand Humberto. And I don't know why Emilio lets him treat him that way. Sandy goes on and on about what a beautiful soul Humberto is and that he's just lost. Well, maybe so, but that doesn't change how I feel about him.

The next morning Puma instructs us to shower with Agua de Florida and make sure we put a lot on our heads. He claims there was too much noise in the room last night. But that wasn't all there was. I'm furious at Puma for allowing Humberto to hijack the ceremony just because he's the one who pays him.

I see right into Puma's weakness; he's afraid of authority.

chapter sixty-one

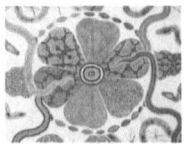

Humberto decides we should have a going-away party. So, Sandy and I take the moto-taxi into Iquitos. We stop by the market to buy supplies for the party. On the way, she asks if I would mind having lunch with Humberto. Hell no!! I don't want to spend any more time in town than I have to, especially with him.

The barrage of smells, noises, and people's energy pummels me, leaving me emotionally bruised and sensitive.

We stop by the Internet cafe to check our emails, which turns out to be a bad idea.

I haven't received even one email from Doug. I'm angry and then sad that I put so much time into the relationship and it failed anyway. Sandy comments, "At least you got out before you're forty!"

I guess this is a sign I need to let go, for good.

Sandy and I buy all the food and drinks, including a bottle of rum and beer.

Humberto comes over to the casita right before the party. I don't want to be around his energy and bombastic tendencies, so I go to the dining hall to see what's going on. I'm ravenous. It's after eight o'clock already, and I distract myself with setting up the rum punch bowl. I'm feeling overwhelmed with all the people, so I hide in the kitchen and talk with Juanita.

In the meantime, table and chairs are pushed to the periphery, converting the dining area into a dance hall. A family from Jan Chama lugs in their stereo system along with one speaker and a car battery to power it. The music selection consists of a single warped cassette tape. It contains Peruvian *cumbia* and American music from the 1980s.

I watch Puma and Humberto.

I almost feel sorry for Puma as he stands next to Humberto with arms crossed, enduring his monologue for hours. I get impatient and casually circle them a few times.

Bored. I seek out Sandy. "How long is Puma going to ignore me?" I whine. "He's been ignoring me for days!"

"What do you expect, considering you rejected him?" She snorts. "Not only that, but you told Humberto what he did, too."

"Well, I thought he should know since he's supposed to be running a healing center!"

I'm about ready to go back to the casita. I have reached my tolerance for music that takes me back to my high school days.

From across the room, Puma and Humberto shake hands and part ways. Puma goes to the table set up with the drinks and food and picks up a couple of plastic glasses and a bottle of beer. He brings them over to me, pouring me a glass of beer. After a few sips, the alcohol surges through my brain. Puma invites me to dance, but I get bored of the jungle shuffle and tell him I'm tired and going to bed. But, mostly I'm pissed off and wallowing in self-pity for being ignored for so long.

I go to bed, but I can't fall asleep. I finally do after the party finishes, the music dies down, and Sandy returns to the casita.

I've been in a pissy-fury for several days since Humberto gave the fire arcana.

The next day I wake up, still fiery.

And I'm not sure who I want to be mad at more, Humberto or Puma.

chapter sixty-two

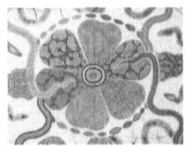

I'm not willing to walk all the way to the swamp and see if Puma is in his casita.

Instead, I go to the kitchen to see if anyone knows of his whereabouts. Juanita arches an eyebrow before telling me he's probably resting under the palapa.

I tiptoe up to the uneven stick fence that encloses the palapa. There he is, swinging in the hammock with his transistor radio up to his ear.

"Can we talk?"

He turns off his radio, "*Si.*" He wriggles a little to the right and pats the taut sisal.

I get in the scratchy hammock next to him with my feet pointing the opposite direction of his.

Nervous, I jump right into the conversation. "What were you and Humberto talking about for so long?"

"We talked about how things aren't good around here. I'm in charge of the guests when everyone leaves the premises. I am the only one here with you. That's not my responsibility." He explains and then takes a long pause before he continues.

"He also told me you said I put a spell on you. I don't do that. You can't get love that way because that isn't love from God."

Whatever!

I wonder what God has to do with anything. Maybe I lost something in translation. All I know is that for sure he put a spell on me.

But I don't care anymore.

I stare at him for a few moments.

I love his laugh, his smile with all the chrome. I have never seen a face like his before. His skin as soft as suede. His eyes intense as arrow tips.

It is then, I finally admit to myself that I really do like him.

chapter sixty-three

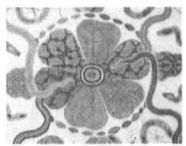

I can't believe my time here is nearly up.

And tonight is our final ayahuasca ceremony.

We will be drinking a new batch of brew made up of several plants, including ayahuasca, chacruna, *pion negro*, and coca leaves.

I get explosively sick. Probably from the party. But I don't feel like my mind is being ripped apart and my body dying. My body now remains generally pretty calm. I manage not to squirm and wiggle the whole time.

Puma does some interesting things in the ceremony. He asks us to hold the Bible open in our hands and breathe in the smell of the pages three times. When it is my turn, I re-open the Bible to a random page. Instantly, I'm downloading codes. The information floods me in the form of lighted Egyptian hieroglyphs.

Earlier in the ceremony, images of the Sphinx pulsated in front of my eyes. I saw bright shiny gold with some blue-colored paint on it. I don't know half the meaning of a lot of stuff I see, but I get the sense that it is some sort of memory I'm integrating.

At one point, Puma is singing in front of me. The moment he put his hand on the top of my head, I feel the need to sit up very straight. It feels as if he is putting a crown on my head. I get the impression that he is preparing me for something.

Sandy, Gavin, Marcos, and I join hands. We create a circle around Puma who is in the middle singing icaros. My body hums with the electricity flowing through it.

My clammy hand holds Sandy's. I lean over, "I have to sit down. I think I'm about to faint."

She says into my ear, "It's the little girl part of you that can't handle the energy. It's the part that was abandoned, it can't take the energy." I give her a "huh" before I sit down on the floor.

Then she says something to Marcos about always trying to get attention. She can be mean.

A vision of Doug comes to me. He's covered in a thick grayish-brown smog sort of like goo. On his back, he has a hunch-back mound. Curious, I go around behind his back, and I see a yellowish-neon-purple energy curled up inside the hump.

Later I tell Puma about what I have seen around Doug. He tells me what he had seen. He says that Doug is sick in his heart and his mind. And that is why the relationship would never work.

I already know that in my gut.

After the ceremony finishes, we all stand outside in the warm night air. Puma comes over to me and gives me a tender hug and a kiss on the lips in front of Gavin, Marcos, and Sandy. I'm a bit embarrassed and flattered at the same time.

Even though it is way after midnight, we aren't tired. Sandy, Gavin, and I decide to escort Marcos back to his hut at the end of the swamp, one last time. A naked transparency bonds us for experiencing this profound life-changing journey together. The flashlight's silver beams bounce off tree limbs, morphs into arms, embracing us on the path.

The gentle padding of rubber boots draws nearer.
Puma catches up.
Encircling his arm around my waist, he pulls me close.

chapter sixty-four

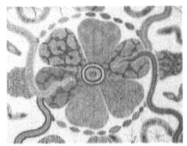

As soon as I'm honest with myself, that I like Puma, the doubts and fears start to surface.

I notice that he has been walking to Jan Chama in the middle of the afternoon with his gold chain on. He doesn't wear that chain any other time. I wonder if he has a *puta* there, a whore. He doesn't seem the type. But you never know. Considering what ayahuasca does to the hormones. He might like the challenge of me and have a puta, as a regular thing.

Sometimes, I don't know if Puma is for real.

I have contradictory evidence.

Or am I finding evidence to fit my story of abandonment and betrayal?

He told me one time he gave the water boys a ten *Nuevo Soles* tip. *Sole* is the Peruvian currency which is around three times less than the U.S. dollar. He told Sandy he also gave the same person five Soles.

One day, I was admiring a ring on his finger. It had a pretty, blue cut-glass stone in it, so he took it off his finger and gave it to me. He said it was, *pura plata*, pure silver. But when I was in the shower the soap rubbed off most of the silver and revealed the ring was copper, leaving my finger green.

chapter sixty-five

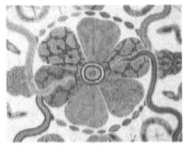

This morning after breakfast I trek out to the swamp to say goodbye to Marcos.

He sees me arriving from down the path. "Hola!"

"Hi, Marcos. I came to bring you the rest of my Maca root powder. You might need it if want to survive the next few months out here." I tease him.

Laughing, "Not very bloody funny," he says in his cockney accent, "It looks like Puma gave you an apology."

Puzzled, furrowing the wrinkle between my eyebrows, "What do you mean?"

"The hug and kiss in front of us last night."

I glance down, slightly embarrassed. "Oh, you think so?"

"Yes," he smirks. "Definitely."

"It's a bit late," I say briskly, covering up my happiness.

"What time are you guys leaving today?"

"Around three. Our flight out of Iquitos is just after five this afternoon."

"Well, I've enjoyed chatting with you and having your company around. It can get pretty lonely out here."

"Good luck with your dieta. And email me when you get home and tell me how it went."

We step towards each other. I wrap my arms around his waist and lay my head across his collarbone.

"You've been a good friend to me, Marcos."

He gives me a tight squeeze and pushes me out at arm's length.

"I'll see you at the entrance, to say good-bye."

"Thanks, Marcos," I say, as I go out the door.

"Hurry and close the door. The mosquitoes!"

I laugh and walk down the wooden steps and put on my anaconda boots.

I see Puma through the screen window, swinging in the hammock, lazily pushing off the wall to keep it moving. He sees me walk up the path to his hut.

"Hola," I wave.

He stops swinging and gets out of his hammock to open the door.

"I came by to give you this." I open my hand, revealing my crystal star necklace.

His eyes light up, and he takes it carefully from my palm. He holds it up by the silver chain and brings it closer to his face. He squints a bit. Still not satisfied he reaches for his blue glasses and puts them on.

His eyes brighten even more as he smiles.

"Muchas gracias." He says, and he leans in to kiss my cheek. "Have a seat."

I sit down in the creaky chair under the window. But the hammock divides the room, making me feel far away from him. I move the chair closer to where he sits on the bed. He places a warm hand on my knee. My skin tingles and I feel heat flood my entire body. I don't move and pretend his touch isn't affecting me. He runs his hand slowly over my cotton capris inching up my inner thighs. I react by grabbing his hand in mine and holding it tight. He withdraws and places it back on the bed.

"Do you want to sit in the hammock?" he invites.

I see the worker-boys outside the window. They carry buckets of water up the ladder to fill up the water tank on the roof. I wave at them since they are looking in. There is no privacy, with only screens for the windows.

"I'm okay here," I tell him. We continue talking. I relax a bit with the laughter and our easy banter.

One of the boys removes the ladder from outside the window, hoisting it up to his shoulder he carries it away. The other one has the bucket in hand.

Puma shouts out the window, "Gracias."

They respond, *"De nada."* as if it is really nothing, carrying fifty gallons of water up a ladder.

"Chao, chao," Puma says

He senses I feel more at ease and edges out another invitation to join him in the hammock. This time I accept.

He climbs in first, reclining back on the cotton, offering me a hand. I miss it as the hammock is swinging away from me. I bust out with nervous laughter. He extends his leg to brake against the wall. I awkwardly place my seat on the swinging hammock, nearly falling out. We burst into laughter. This time I grab the fabric with both hands to steady myself and I crawl in more easily and nestle between his thighs. A few seconds later I feel his penis hardening and pulsing against my back.

I don't know if I should get out or not. This is way more than talking. Barely breathing, I try to not move and cause him further excitement. But it's too late.

He relocates his hands to my belly. He lets them rest there a short while. He seems to know when I've acclimated to him before he dares to explore further. Almost with invisible movement, his hands migrate up to my chest. Gently, with the back of his hand, he draws an infinity sign around each breast.

I can hardly stand it.

I'm going to explode with desire.

Then he stops. Like migrating birds, his lips rove across my neck. I turn my head to meet them. We kiss briefly.

"Te quiero mucho." I love you a lot, he tells me.

I don't respond. Part of me is flattered. Part of me thinks it's the usual ploy so that I will give in and have sex with him.

He places his hand on my abdomen. Testing my strength, he slides his hands, centimeter by centimeter ever closer. Until his fingers eventually find their way to my mound. I rapidly pull them off and hold his arms crossed over my body so tightly until the burning fire diminishes.

He whispers in my ear, "I want to lick between the wings of your *paloma*."

"No!" I shriek, perhaps sounding a little too panicked. My heart is pounding, and I realize I'm not breathing. I take a few long, slow breaths to gather my wits.

His relentless fingers travel south again. I'm as curious about my reaction as he probably is so I let him linger longer each time before yanking his hands off my body. His touch is like an ocean wave on a breezy day. It contains enough pressure to entice pleasure and is not forceful at all. Every time he touches me those waves build with intensity until I can hardly stand the tension.

"You have a lot of resistance," he comments.

"Because I don't want to lose control."

This must sound like an invitation, for he says, "I want to use my tongue all over your soft white skin."

I haven't had anyone do that in a really long time. He's trying every angle until he can break me, forcing me to endure further torture.

I think, *he would be a very passionate lover*. His touch is gentle and confident. *He might actually know what he is doing. Maybe that comes with age and experience.*

"Let's move to the bed," he suggests.

"No." I quickly add to soften the rejection, "What time is it?" I twist his wrist so I can see the face on his watch. I've been here with him two and a half hours!

"I leave in an hour. I have to go and pack!" I slip out of the hammock with him following behind. He leaves me on the steps with a kiss on the cheek.

Inside, Sandy lies on her bed, writing in her journal.

She stops when I walk over to the table where my backpack waits. I quickly roll up my leftover t-shirts and capris. I gave away a few shirts and my clunky anaconda boots. I gather up the crystals from the altar and stow them in my medicine bag. I carefully wrap the piranha teeth in a sock and place my altar cards between the pages of my journal.

"You're not packed yet," I say stating the obvious.

"Yeah, I know. I've decided to stay another week."

I look at her a moment. I'm angry. *She could have told me earlier.* It doesn't make much sense to me since she has to pay a change fee for her ticket plus an extra week to stay here.

Then she adds, "I could use more medicine."

And I bet she is still thinking about convincing Humberto how great they'd be together.

I push my anger aside. I pick up the tin, partially filled with candle wax.

"Do you want my candles?"

"Yeah, that would be great."

I leave them on the altar.

"Are you going to be okay by yourself?" Gavin is leaving in a couple of days, and Marcos keeps to himself.

"I'll be fine. Don't worry. I'm not going to die, if that is what you're worried about!"

She still looks like a skeleton to me but not quite as yellow. I'm mad at her for deciding to stay.

The moto-taxi waits for me, along with Marcos, Gavin, Juanita, the worker-boys, Maria, Humberto, Puma, and Sandy. I give everyone a big hug.

When its Puma's turn he hugs me and kisses my cheek, whispering in my ear, "Be careful, my love."

Lastly, I give Sandy a hug, "Take care of yourself and get out of here if it gets too crazy!" I advise.

"I'll be fine. I'll see you in a week!'

chapter sixty-six

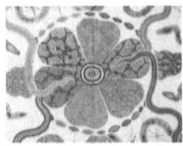

I check my email at the airport in Lima.
Still no word from Doug.

He must be trying hard to disconnect from me. That makes it easier, I guess.

After an all-night flight from Lima, I feel exhausted.

Fortunately, I don't have to wait long for the shuttle to take me to the long-term parking lot to get my car. I hope I remember how to drive it.

These past three weeks feel longer than a lifetime.

I wrinkle my nose up at the funky smell. I look around for its source and realize Sandy left her coffee cup in the cup holder. I have an hour drive home. I roll down a window, tossing the algae-looking coffee onto the pavement.

And no, I didn't forget how to drive.

Oddly enough I no longer need music to entertain me; my mind still remains peaceful. A pang hits my heart as I notice how brown and stark the high desert is. I miss the nurturing greens of the jungle already.

The house is vacant and catacomb-cold. My spider plant has a flat, stepped-on look from dehydration. It appears as if Doug hasn't been here. I reach for the phone.

"Georgina, I just wanted to let you know I moved back up to my mom's house," he says apologetically, "I think we need some space."

I swallow down the lump of hurt that has climbed up from my heart.

I don't know why.

We had been separated once before for several months and then got back together, and it didn't work.

Why would I think now would be any different? Because I am different?

Like a loud thunder-like clap, Mama Naila's previous words pierce through my questions and reverberate inside my head. They transport me back to the awkwardness of my time in Zanzibar.

"What is going on with you?" Mama Naila asked. I looked at her as she continued, "You've put on a lot of weight, and you look puffy now."

This isn't helping, I thought. I don't respond, so she goes on.

"Why are you so downtrodden? You are nothing like you were before."

I wanted to confess to her my guilt about my affair with Sunley. And that was why Doug and I were acting strangely. I wanted to tell her about all that had led up to my decision. I wanted to tell her about feeling abandoned and unloved by his mother and my mother. I wanted her to feel as sorry for me as I did for myself. I wanted her on my side as if there were sides on who to like more. But, I really just wanted her to hold me in those big strong arms and stroke my hair with a mother's tenderness until I could feel peace settle in my heart.

Instead, she said, "Why do you beg for the crumbs he throws on the floor?"

Insulted, I didn't know what to say. I denied those pinching words for a long time.

I'm not like that at all! I told myself.

But what she said still haunts me.

chapter sixty-seven

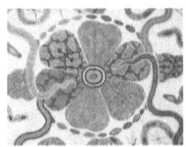

My around-the-world island fantasy didn't fix my marriage.

Ayahuasca didn't fix it either.

We had done all the things couples are supposed to do; go to counseling, spend more quality time together, communicate better. Honestly, by this point, I just don't have it in me anymore to want to make it work. But I don't know that at the time.

I am worn out.

I blamed him for everything that went wrong. How controlling and dominating he was. How he didn't love me. When he stopped loving me.

But in Peru, I realized I needed something different in my life. He and I are two separate universes eclipsing each other.

I need more zest in my life.

I don't want to be one of those people with vacant eyes who act as if life got the better of them.

I need to stop flat-lining.

The hollow house is so silent without him. I don't know what to do with myself in all that quietness. I make a fire and sit staring at the dancing orange and cobalt flames. I don't know what else to do. I'm numb. And oddly, free. I'm not sure what I'm supposed to do. I think if I keep looking into the fire the answer about what to do next will jump out of the flames and ignite my mind.

That night, I have a dream of Puma.

He is leading the ceremony and sings icaros for me. I have a big hole inside; I miss the deep connection I had felt during ceremony. I feel him thinking of me. Early the next morning the phone rings. Pressing the green talk button, I hear a string of Spanish words.

"Puma, *despacio por favor!*" Slow down, please! I don't understand when he talks so fast without cues from body language to help me out. I get a couple words in edgewise before he tells me he will call in a few days and hangs up.

My stomach flutters; butterfly wings tickle my insides. A yearning wells up from the depths of my being. I feel a desperate need to change everything in my life, and now!

I got a kick in the pants from the ayahuasca. I feel so motivated. I know I can't keep living my life the way it has been for so long. I realize it is killing me, my soul. The jungle awoke the juices within me. My spirit is ablaze and awake.

Reaching under the kitchen sink, I pull out the box of black plastic trash bags.

Ripping a couple off the roll, I march to the bedroom closet. Violently yanking Doug's clothes off their hangers, I stuff them into the bags and pile them out in the hallway. Armed with a few more trash bags, I venture into Doug's office. I pull the draws out from his desk, dumping all his miscellaneous papers and crap directly into the bags. From the garage, I select a few boxes for his books and cull them from the shelves. My last step: removing his mother's mausoleum of watercolor paintings from the walls.

I take a three-sixty of the room, satisfied I've gotten most of the visible relics out of my sight.

I load everything up into my Subaru.

Overstuffed with black plastic, I drive to my friend Roberta's house. On the way, I call her to see if she will join me on the drop-off mission. I lack the courage to face Doug if he happens to be there. Gladly she accompanies me, and she lets me rant on the way to his house. Fortunately, he's not there.

At lightning speed, we unload the car and drop everything in a giant heap right outside the front door, making sure to inconvenience him as much as possible.

Laughing like naughty school girls, we jump into the car. Roberta and I decide to go for breakfast at a nearby coffee shop down on Baca street. I tell her about my Peruvian adventures and all about Puma.

"Your eyes have this, look at me," she instructs, turning my chin in her direction. "Yes, they have a glitter in them, all sparkly!" I smile, a little self-conscious. "And, there is something more," she's trying to put her finger on it. "It's in your aura. Umm. Yes! You appear confident, more certain." She takes a sip of her Moroccan mint tea, "How was everything with Sandy?"

"We had our ups and downs, but overall it went okay." I didn't want to reveal all the dirty details. "She wanted to stay a week longer. So I returned by myself."

chapter sixty-eight

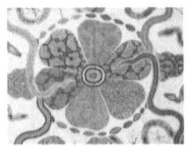

The week flew past while I wait for Sandy's return.
She has been home only a couple of days before I can no longer resist the urge to see her and hear of her adventures at the healing center.

Plum circles nestle around her eyes. *She looks exhausted*, I think when she opens the door for me. I step inside to the warmth of a roaring fire.

Her half-unpacked olive-green backpack lays on the floor. She rummages through it and extracts a small blue plastic bag. She hands it to me; peeking inside I glimpse several red and black beaded necklaces made of *huaydura* seeds and a crumpled piece of paper. I notice Sandy looking out the corner of her eye at me as I open the note,

"*Te amo mucho, cuidate mi carino. Regresame muy pronto.* I love you, take care, my dear. Return to me soon. Puma" Written in child-like printing. I smile at his sentiment.

"I got the same thing," Sandy says. "But I didn't get a note. What did he say?"

I repeat the message.

Curious about Puma's feelings for me, "Did he behave himself?" I ask jokingly.

With a pained look on her face, she says, "He cares for you very much. You are all he talks about."

In that moment, I am a bird that has crashed into a glass window; stunned and shivering.

I dismiss it as one of my silent fears.

A week later, Sandy and I meet for coffee at the Santa Fe Baking Company. It's crowded as usual, but we manage to find a table squeezed in the middle of the restaurant. I feel something invisible coming from Sandy that doesn't feel good to me.

"Everything was red with blood, and we were both covered in it." She starts telling me about her dream, "I don't know if this is a past-life thing or what." She says. Her eyes brim with tears, "I slept with him. I am so sorry." This comes tumbling out onto my lap. "It was awful." she pauses a second. "And all he wants is you!"

Shocked, I stare into the back of her pooling blue eyes, looking for her soul so I won't hate her and rip her hair out in public. It takes a few moments to locate the part of her I love, but it has shrunk to the size of one of those huaydura seeds.

"Why?" I want to know. "You are my best friend. You are my sister. You know how I felt about him! Why would you do that to me?"

"I just got so lonely there without you. And Puma was there. Humberto left, and I never saw him again. It was just Puma and me most of the time. I didn't want to feel so alone." She cried. "I am so sorry." She went further to explain the act itself and how he left immediately afterward to go back to his hut, in the swamp, at the other end of the property. "I felt so used and disgusted."

Well good for you! You deserve to feel that way!

"He really is in love with you. He doesn't love me at all. I couldn't make him love me," she tries explaining.

Just then, in a moment of disbelief in addition to the betrayal and disgust festering under my skin, I see this woman, a soul sister and my best friend, as weak and pathetic. I can no longer see her strength nor respect her. I don't even want to be next to her. Coldness claims my heart. My eyes lose their warmth. I glare deep into her eyes, she looks down to her fingers fidgeting in her lap.

My smile fake, I say, "I forgive you because you are my sister," I say icily. "I won't forgive him. He's not worth my time."

And the canyon between us grows.

A cyclone of fatigue whips around me and engulfs me in a black sticky tar that oozes into the center of my being. I feel a thousand pounds. And yet I have a lightness of clarity. I continue looking at Sandy, wondering if I will feel sorry for her. But all I can think of is how I want my bed.

I'm tired of letting people treat me cruelly. I'm tired of people treating me like a doormat because I want them to like me. I'm tired of people thinking I will take their shit and abuse because that is what I usually do. I'm tired of not loving myself enough to stand up for myself.

I am so fucking tired.

I just want to go home.

I reach behind me, taking my blue North Face down vest off the back of the chair. Getting up, I slip my arms methodically through each arm hole and pull the zipper up to my chin. The solid wooden chair scrapes the cement floor as I push it under the table.

I put my hands deep inside my pockets and walk away.

chapter sixty-nine

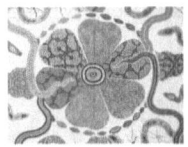

Submerged in my sarcophagus-like tub, I sink further into those inky thoughts that knot me up.

We got divorced April 9, 2008, and it was about as unceremonious as getting married in the courthouse.

The hardest part was putting the pen on the paper and signing my name. I had hesitated, pretending I was working up to a grand signature. This would be it, the death of my life as I had known it.

The idea of freedom terrifies me.

And, no going back once I made my mark. A flash of fear ran through me and brought on a cold sweat.

I had the delusion our divorce would be similar, short and sweet because we hadn't the complication of kids. But, it still got nasty. How much money went where, who got what thing. And Willie, our dog, there was no fight over him, but it broke my heart, knowing he would no longer be in my life. It's funny in a twisted sort of way, how the only thing left in a divorce when the love has flown away, are things. Who wants to hang onto what and how money is the final indicator of who won, who had more power in the relationship. And who made the greatest sacrifice.

Hollowness fills my insides. I have nothing but a handful of items. *Am I nothing?* I don't feel my worth, my value. No one truly loves me. I doubt that anyone ever would. Self-destruction and uncontrollable rage choke me. I want to die to all this pain. And, die to this shell of a human I have become.

Numbness creeps into my frozen talons curled around the black knife handle.

Utterly hopeless, I don't see any reason to live.

Bubbles slowly escape through my silent scream.

Like a selfish child filled with self-pity, I demand an explanation, "God, whoever! What is going on? I don't know what to do to get rid of this pain."

I decide to give God one more chance, pleading, "Give me a definite sign that my life has meaning. That I have a purpose. Give me a clear and definite sign that there is more to this life. Give me a reason to live!"

I dare God to prove me wrong.

Brriinng, brriinng.

Muffled, I hear something through my water-clogged ears.

Confused, I focus more, unwilling to relinquish my watery tomb.

Shit.

The phone is ringing! It's way past midnight. Someone must have died. Nobody calls this late unless its bad news.

I burst through the water's surface, gasping, dropping the knife with a steely clang on the creamy-white tile. I grab a towel from the counter and skate down the hallway. My hands pulsate, adrenaline prickling beneath my skin.

I lunge at the phone sitting on the counter. I pick up the receiver, and I hold it the way you would a delicate china teacup.

"Hello?" I answer shakily, expecting a Canadian accent from home telling me the grave news.

"*Hola?* Are you all right, *mi amor?*" I hear the concerned voice.

"I was so worried about you. I was in ceremony, and I saw you in such pain. You have too much *cholera*, rage. I called as soon as I finished," he says lightening fast.

His words jump-start my heart.

How could he feel me thousands of miles away when my own husband couldn't feel me in the same house? When I can't even feel me, inside my own body?

A dam releases. Tears gush down my cheeks.

I choke out, "I'm okay, now."

"*Gracias a Dios*, thank God," responds his fatigued voice. "I need to get to my bed now. I will call you tomorrow, *mi amor*. Goodnight, *mi amor*, goodnight."

Click.

His voice lingers like a fine mist before it falls into the darkness.

Tears still stream down my sodden cheeks.

I look up as if that is where God must live. I don't know where he lives. But tonight, I had evidence someone listened, even to my small voice. Somehow, I knew my life mattered. And that was enough for now.

On my way to my bedroom, I walk down the hallway. Moonlight bouncing off the white walls, I enter the bathroom.

I lower my hand into the tepid water and pull the plug.

I stand a moment, watching water spiral down the vortex. I lean over to blow out the beeswax candle, inhaling the sweet buttery smoke as it whispers around my head, vanishing into the night.

In a pang of shame, I pick up the lifeless metal knife and turn it over nimbly in my hand. The very thing that might have taken my life away. Like poison oak, I brush it away from me, it tumbles, clattering next to the sink.

I walk through the door.

I turn around, facing it.

With one hand on the handle, I pull it shut and walk away, leaving the pain inside.

Oddly, a profound sense of peace and calm cocoons me. There is a higher purpose for me and my life. I don't understand what it is but I trust that I am guided and protected to fulfill something greater than me.

He did call early the next morning.

"Puma," I said, "I'm coming to Peru."

coming soon...

The Shaman's Lover Trilogy

Book II

the Shattering

www.theShamansLover.com

about the author

Georgina Kemm is a guardian of bees, ten chickens, two hound dogs, numerous plants, flowers and trees. She facilitates Women's Sacred Medicine Immersions and Creative Heart Writing Retreats in New Mexico and Peru. *The Spell* is the first book in *The Shaman's Lover Trilogy*, a memoir based upon her apprenticeship and life-changing misadventures with a Peruvian shaman. Georgina lives in New Mexico with her beloved, Damian.

Find out more about Georgina's books and Women's Sacred Medicine Immersions: www.theShamansLover.com

10% of book sales will be donated to replenish the Amazon with trees, medicinal plants and for educational purposes: non-profit, *Asociación Los Cielos Raenanti* (Peru) 575-2017. www.loscielosperu.com/the-sanctuary

www.ingramcontent.com/pod-product-compliance
Lightning Source LLC
Chambersburg PA
CBHW030441090526
44586CB00044B/488